Cruising Connecticut

With a Picnic Basket

2nd Edition

by Jan Mann

Jan Mann

Hillside House Publishing
Connecticut

Cruising Connecticut with a Picnic Basket

Credits:

Book Design: Civic Design at the Hartford Art School/University of Hartford

Creative Direction: Nancy Wynn

Designers: Tim Bayon, Ron Pezzullo and Brendan Sullivan

Production: Ron Pezzullo

Illustrations: Tim Bayon and Brendan Sullivan

Cartoon characters: Jim Wagner

Author photograph: Michele Colletti

Additional photographs:

(with the exception of page 18) by author

ISBN 978-0-9777174-1-5
Printed in the United States of America

Professional Recipes:

"Crab and Crackers" by Eunice Naomi Wiebolt, author of *Cooking With Confidence*, Published by Romarin Publishing Co., Page 20

"Chicken Caprese" by Les Harris, Glastonbury Gourmet, Page 21

"Gazpacho" by Metro Bis Restaurant co-owner, Chef Christopher Prosperi, Page 24

"Joe's Jambalaya" by Joe Cahn, Commissioner of Tailgating, Page 52

"Vegan Peanut Butter-Chocolate Chip Cookies" by Erin Schuh, Page 69

"Halibut en Papillote with Pesto" by Chef Richard Moriarty, Center for Culinary Arts, Page 72

New "Cold Lobster Salad Roll" by Adam Alderin, Chef of Max Fish, Page 104

"Almond Macaroons" by the late Ellen Bowen, courtesy of Pam Russo, Site Manager, Roseland Cottage, Page 106

"Wild Mushroom and Oyster Chowder" by Maggie Jones, Executive Director, Denison Pequotsepos Nature Center, Page 130

"Deviled Crab Stuffed Eggs" by Star Mader, Page 138

New "A Spanish Tapas Picnic" by Prudence Sloane, Radio & TV Food Show Host, Page 216

To my loving family,

Karen, Rob, Kylie & Andy Hoke
Holly, Kevin, Joseph, Brendan & Mikayla McCarthy

Michele, Tom, Ally, Cassie & C.J. Colletti

Thanks for joining me on day trips
(let's not stop just because the book is finished)
and for the agreeable tasting of new recipes
even knowing they were not all going to be perfect.

Acknowledgments

My love and gratitude to the following people who accompanied me in this extraordinary odyssey — many were with me for the entire journey, some joined me at different locations along the way, and others hopped on board just recently. It matters not the length of the trip, but that the presence of each one has made the journey more significant.

To my three daughters, who have been incredible companions on the Cruising Connecticut journey, and the journey of life:

. . . Karen, for her expert editing. Along with this awesome task, came wise advice and ingenious suggestions that made my writing the best it can be. Wasn't it just a short time ago when I was proofreading her work? I couldn't be happier that the tables have turned . . . Holly, who joined me in the early days of cruising (what fun!), then went home to create special recipes for the occasion, and more recently, advised, tested, and proofread final recipes, all with zeal and dedication . . . Michele, who always remembered to ask how the book was coming along, then took the time to listen to my joys and woes; I thank her for the brainstorming sessions on art and design, and assistance with a myriad of pre- and post-production matters.

To good friends who offered recipes, ideas and support; and especially to Bonye Barone, Terry Bernard, Deborah Dierman, Fran Maddaluno, Aili Singer, and my sister and friend, Pat Kirwin, who collectively kept me company on day trips, shared, created, tested, and tasted recipes and provided wonderful hours of creative discussions; and to Linda Rohlfs, who critiqued every chapter and cheered me on while highlighting her favorite passages with a purple marker.

To my coach, Joan Gleckler, for both personal and professional assistance. Her reassurances and expertise were invaluable during what, at times, seemed like overwhelming tasks; and to Sheryl Quesnel, for guiding me through the maze of printing options.

I also thank Diane Wright Hirsch, RD, MPH, for writing the food safety section; the knowledgeable folks at the tourist attractions who shared helpful information and recipes; and the chefs, "Wife of the Chef," and other food industry professionals, who not only contributed wonderful recipes but also shared related tidbits and valuable suggestions.

▶ Contents

"What I set down here is true until someone else passes that way and rearranges the world in his own style."

Travels with Charley by John Steinbeck

There may be times when it will be prudent to call ahead to confirm that the information stated in this book is still accurate.

Introduction

Dear Readers,

We rely on the information in travel books to be as current and accurate as possible, so I recently grabbed my picnic basket and crisscrossed the state to revisit my favorite places. It's amazing how much can change in a couple of years and I am happy to share these changes with you.

The most common were new hours and admission prices, with a few picnic areas that had been redesigned or enhanced, and a winery that changed hands and was being renovated. I also discovered new attractions at some of the old places. Just two examples are Gillette's recently refurbished electric engine from his miniature railroad, and a charming boat trip added to the Essex chapter.

As I cruised around the state, I experienced the same sense of adventure that prompted me to write the First Edition. In fact, I had so much fun that I just kept going, adding two new day trips and picnics to this edition. One is the Mark Twain House & Museum in Hartford, and the other is Gouveia Vineyards in Wallingford.

Here is what readers can expect to find in this 2nd Edition of Cruising Connecticut:

▸ The original 40 day trips and picnicking information with complete updates.

▸ The same great recipes as in the First Edition.

▸ Two brand new destinations. And, wait until you taste the exciting celebrity recipes that accompany these new day trips!

By the way, my website now includes a page for updated information and changes to destinations as I learn about them. Be sure to check from time to time: www.cruisingconnecticut.com.

Happy Cruising,

Jan Mann

Each Day Trip is Divided into three Sections:

The Activity

Connecticut has such an amazing array of things to see and do, my challenge was deciding which activities and destinations to include. I'm still mourning the many favorites I had to leave out in order to obtain versatility in both content and regions within the State.

I tried to select activities that would appeal to every age and interest. And, I wanted to introduce folks to places they might not be familiar with, as well as highlight well-known tourist spots that may have new or revised attractions. The length of time an activity takes also varies, because at times our schedule will allow us to indulge in an entire day of fun, while other times we just need a breather, a two-hour interlude away from the routine in order to get re-energized.

In this section, I share my experiences and observations from each day trip along with any options that may be available. Many times, readers will have a choice to either follow the path described or veer off in a new direction.

The Picnic

Picnics can be elegant or casual, organized or spontaneous, the ultimate social event or a quick lunch break. The key to planning the perfect picnic is not only to consider the occasion or activity, but the available facilities.

Is there a picnic table or lawn to spread out on, or will we be balancing food on our laps while sitting on a bench? Are there charcoal grills for cooking? Will we be picnicking from a backpack or a tailgate? All this information is necessary in order to determine how long and how comfortable our picnic may be, and, perhaps even more important, what we will pack in our picnic basket.

What's In Our Picnic Basket?

The suggested menus are designed to spark ideas for each picnicker's own unique situation and preference. They are varied enough to "mix and match" with selections from other pages.

The featured recipe, or in some cases recipes, are designed to complement the rest of the items in the suggested menu. First and foremost, they had to be versatile (there's my favorite word again), taste great, be simple to prepare, and contain ingredients that are either a staple or easy to find. The final test was how transportable each recipe is, given the ease and accessibility of the picnic site.

With the exception of the beverage recipes, menus contain no drink suggestions, leaving this up to individual preference. But, remember to pack a water bottle when hiking or biking, or doing any strenuous exercise.

As I bring you along on my adventures, I continually refer to "we" and you may wonder who has accompanied me. The "we" is a composite of family, friends, neighbors, and acquaintances, whoever happened to be with me at that particular time. It isn't that I won't go on a day trip alone. I often do when there is no one readily available, or I want to get off by myself to do some research. My preference for these trips, however, was to bring someone along to share the event and offer a new perspective.

I hope you enjoy reading this book, and that it will coax you to get out and spend some time cruising Connecticut. This is exactly what I have been doing for nearly twenty-five years while writing this book. What a ride!

Brookfield Craft Center
Brookfield

I f your interest in crafts is that of an appreciative observer, take a drive to Brookfield Craft Center. If your interest in crafts is that of a serious craftsman, take a drive to Brookfield Craft Center. Creative roads lead to this professional non-profit craft center, for both neophytes and experienced artisans.

We begin our tour at the main building, The Gallery, which contains the Exhibition Hall and Fine Craft Gift Shop. Clearly, the work presented here is of the highest quality. We especially enjoy the versatility of the various mediums, as well as the contrast between functional and decorative items and serious and whimsical items. Numerous American artists are represented, including instructors of the Center's classes and workshops. It is easy to understand why Brookfield Craft Center has been thriving for more than fifty years!

Four charming colonial-style studios are in close proximity to The Gallery, amidst woodsy surroundings, including the Still River. The historic Brookfield Railroad Station, the newest addition to the campus, is across the street. It was recently acquired and renovated for additional studios. Future plans are in place to renovate the existing buildings in order to expand and continue Brookfield's fine craft traditions.

The "Brookfield Craft Center Quarterly" is available at The Gallery and lists close to 100 classes and workshops for adults and teens. Leading artisans from the area and around the country come here to teach traditional crafts, such as pottery, painting, weaving, and jewelry making, as well as more unique offerings like blacksmithing, boat building, paper making, and wood turning. Classes are scheduled year-round during the week and also on

Brookfield Craft Center

Address: 286 Whisconier Road, Route 25, Brookfield, CT 06804.
Telephone: (203) 775-4526.
Website: www. brookfieldcraftcenter.org.
Hours: Mon–Sat 10–5; Sun 12–5. Closed major holidays.
Directions: Exits 9 or 7 off Interstate 84. Located on Route 25, just east of the intersection with Routes 7 & 202.

weekends, making it convenient for people who do not live close by or who have busy work schedules.

Our delightful two-to-three hour interlude includes meandering around the grounds and studios, browsing through the gift shop, and enjoying a leisurely picnic lunch. After lunch, we look through the Craft Center Quarterly and lament the fact that we have just missed the annual September open house, which includes craft demonstrations and studio tours. There is still time, however, for the Holiday Craft Exhibition & Sale scheduled from early November through the end of December.

▶ The Picnic

What a serendipitous discovery—a small patio connected to one of the studios sitting on the banks of the Still River. The small round tables and umbrellas clearly shout, "Picnic!" No one else is outside on this September weekday afternoon, and only the unpacking of our picnic basket and the melodious river flowing amidst the rocks interrupts the quiet.

I have always been fascinated by the origin of names, and perhaps someday I will research how this river (which is anything but "still") got its name. A volunteer does not have the answer, but is able to share something interesting—the Still River is the only river in Connecticut that flows from South to North, in this case to the Housatonic.

After a leisurely lunch and armed with a wish list of fall classes we head home to check our calendars.

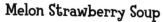

Chef salad

► **Melon Strawberry Soup**

Sugar cookies

Melon Strawberry Soup
(Courtesy of Holly McCarthy)

Soup course—side with salad or sandwich—dessert. Take your pick. This soup will remain chilled for hours so it is a practical yet delicious addition to a summer picnic menu.

1 package (12-ounce) frozen whole strawberries (will only use half)
1 large canataloupe
1 cup orange juice
1/4 cup fresh lime juice
1 tablespoon honey
1 bottle (16-ounce) lemon-lime carbonated beverage

▸ If strawberries are a frozen block, partially thaw, break apart and refreeze.

▸ Remove rinds and seeds from cantaloupe and cut into chunks. Puree in a blender or food processor until smooth. Add orange juice, lime juice, and honey. Whirl until well blended.

▸ Pour into a pitcher and chill for 2 or more hours. Before leaving for your picnic, cut one-half of the frozen strawberries in half and add to soup mixture. Pour into a 2-quart wide mouth thermos to transport to picnic.

▸ To serve, measure 3/4 cup soup into bowl and add 1/4 cup of the carbonated beverage.

▸ Yield: 5-6 one cup servings.

✳ ✳ Fun Alternatives! ✳ ✳

For a festive occasion, replace the carbonated beverage with champagne.

For a little more color during blueberry season, add a few to each bowl.

Downtown Cabaret Theatre
Bridgeport

Picture this! It is a balmy summer evening. You have positioned your folding chair on a spot of sprawling green lawn under a starlit sky. You and your friends are eating the picnic delicacies packed especially for the occasion. Between bites you are listening to a band / concert / performer / play (choose one). Now the picture is complete.

But, wait … what if, instead of a balmy summer evening, it is a rainy fall evening, and rather than a starlit sky, there is a chandelier overhead. You are sitting at a round table with a red tablecloth and you don't have to worry about the weather or the ants or even if it's summer. At Downtown Cabaret Theatre, you can enjoy a picnic and fine theater year-round.

The form of entertainment known as the "Cabaret" (café and concert combined) evolved from minstrels and strolling players in Paris, to more serious performing art in Munich, to Vaudeville in Bridgeport, Connecticut. The year was 1976.

In the mid-eighties, we attended our first show at Downtown Cabaret. *Wop-Bop a-Loo-Bop a-Loop Bam-Boom!* was an original production celebrating music of the 50s and 60s. We were hooked. Live professional theater and picnicking are an unbeatable combination, and to my knowledge, there is no other such venue in Connecticut.

The Theatre continues to present musicals, both original and Broadway productions, such as *The King and I*, *The Buddy Holly Story*, and *Grease*. Our most recent show is *Hair*, which is every bit as impressive and fun as the Wop-Bop we enjoyed years before.

Downtown Cabaret Theatre

Address: 263 Golden Hill Street, Bridgeport, CT 06604.
Telephone: Administration (203) 576-1634 Box Office (203) 576-1636.
Website: www.dtcab.com.
Hours: Tues–Fri 10–3.
Ticket price: Varies.
Directions: May be obtained from website or box office. Park in a guarded lot right across the street from the theatre for $2 per car.

Note:
Downtown Cabaret Theatre is currently undergoing changes in its production schedule. At this time, Cabaret Nights and Children's Theatre will have regularly scheduled performances; Musicals are expected to be offered intermittently during the year. Check the website regularly for current offerings.

Many of the shows are suitable for the entire family, but be sure to check the schedule for the Downtown Cabaret Children's Company, featuring weekend matinee performances of the best-loved classics. It is certain that no one will be more enthusiastic about the combination of indoor theater and a picnic than children.

Courtesy of Downtown Cabaret Theatre

▶ The Picnic

Having no idea what to expect during our first indoor theater picnic, we have a choice—either ask a lot of questions beforehand, or simply wing it. The decision is to wing it, including Buffalo chicken wings.

Wrong choice! We learn the hard way that wings should be eaten in the light. Since we are in total darkness when the show begins, we must figure out a way to maneuver the wings, first to the bowl of dip that they long for and then to our eager mouths. Let's just say it's a good thing we have plenty of napkins, and we won't even mention the sight of the tablecloth once the lights come on. There is only one part of our menu that works really well, and that is the basket of fresh fruit we brought to double as a centerpiece!

By the second visit, we are seasoned in the art of picnicking at Downtown Cabaret. We arrive when the Theatre opens, one-half hour before the performance, which is when the majority of theater-goers arrive. After finding our seats, unpacking the cooler and picnic basket, and pouring a glass of wine, we enjoy our picnic amidst a boisterous crowd and a wonderfully lit room. As the lights dim and the show is about to start, we are almost finished and can easily continue eating the last delicious bites of dinner without any mishaps. In fact, the first thing I notice when the lights come on during intermission is that the tablecloth is still spotless. A proud moment!

The rule for picnic fare at Downtown Cabaret seems to be that anything goes. Folks walk in with everything from a large tray of fresh shrimp to take-out sandwiches (a snack bar in the lobby sells chips, candy, soft drinks, ice and coffee). One couple arrives at our table with Chinese takeout, the containers set in a fancy picnic basket. Classy. Others bring only drinks, saying it is too early for a meal at this 5:30 show and they plan to go to a restaurant for dinner after the show. Privately, I think this would have been a good time to try out my best appetizers.

▸ What's In Our Picnic Basket?

▸ Crab & Crackers
▸ Chicken Caprese
Cold Salad or Slaw
Fresh Pineapple Spears
Chocolate Truffles

Crab & Crackers

The following recipe is excerpted from Cooking With Confidence: Inspirations for Good Food at Home, published by and written permission granted from Romarin Publishing Co., Brainerd, Minnesota. Here's a quick-to-fix version of an old favorite. Served warm (as a dip), or cold (as a spread), you'll agree the taste is always on the money. Choose whole wheat or other hearty crackers to showcase this appetizer.

1 (8-ounce) cream cheese, softened
1/2 cup sour cream
1/4 cup mayonnaise
1 (6-ounce) can crab meat, drained
1/2 cup fresh parsley, minced
2 tablespoons onion, grated
2 large cloves fresh garlic, minced

2 tablespoons sherry or white wine
1 tablespoon Dijon mustard
1/4 teaspoon Old Bay seasoning
1/4 teaspoon bottled hot sauce
1/2 cup slivered almonds
crackers for serving

▸ Preheat oven to 325 degrees.

▸ In a large bowl, combine cream cheese, sour cream, and mayonnaise until mixture is fairly smooth and creamy. Stir in crab meat, parsley, onion, garlic, sherry, mustard, Old Bay, and hot sauce; mix well.

▸ Spoon mixture into a shallow 1-quart baking/serving dish. Sprinkle almonds evenly over the top.

▸ Bake 20 minutes. Turn your oven control from "Bake" to "Broil." Move the dish to the uppermost rack of the oven; broil 2 minutes to brown the almonds. Serve (at any chosen temperature) with your favorite crackers as a dip or spread.

▸ 8-10 appetizer servings.

► Glastonbury Gourmet's Chicken Caprese

Courtesy of Les Harris — Executive Chef @ Glastonbury Gourmet

Chicken Breasts (sliced thin)
Flour
Eggs, Milk
Fresh Tomato
Fresh Ovoline Mozzarella (4 oz. balls)

Balsamic Vinegar (for reduction)
Olive Oil
Salt & Pepper
Fresh Basil

- ► Wash off the chicken breast and pat dry with a clean towel.

- ► Place Balsamic Vinegar in a heavy bottom sauce pan and begin reducing to a thin syrup consistency.

- ► Prepare a flat bottom container for flour. Season flour lightly with salt & pepper. Place chicken (thinly sliced) into flour (both sides) and tap excess flour off the chicken breast.

- ► Place the above chicken breast in an egg wash (beaten eggs with milk). Remove when coated thoroughly and place back into flour (the egg wash acts as glue). Lightly coat each side of chicken with the flour and tap off excess again.

- ► Heat up sauté pan with olive oil and butter. Place chicken into hot pan and sauté both sides until golden brown. Remove from pan and place into a preheated oven (325 degrees) for approximately 7 to 10 minutes (time depends on thickness of chicken). The chicken should be cooked completely.

- ► Place cooked chicken on plate. Slice your tomato and ovoline mozzarella and layer them down the chicken sideways. Add a fresh leaf of basil in between the tomato and ovoline. Sprinkle with salt & pepper to taste.

- ► Drizzle the balsamic vinegar reduction over the above finished chicken and enjoy!

- ► Total time from start to finish is 20 to 30 minutes.

Eugene O'Neill Theater Center
Waterford

Forty years ago, the Eugene O'Neill Theater Center started out as a National Playwrights Conference. Playwrights, both new and experienced, could work in a stimulating and creative environment, accompanied by a staff of professionals who support both playwrights and potential new works for the theater.

From hundreds of applicants, up to fifteen playwrights are invited to the O'Neill each July to work on their plays with the assistance of professional directors, actors, and designers. Each play has only a few days of rehearsals prior to the first of two performances held for the public. The authors are encouraged to make last minute changes to their work-in-progress; therefore, the actors do not memorize their lines, but instead carry scripts while performing. Other than the actors and their scripts, the stage is likely to be bare, unless some modules are added for emphasis.

We feel like we are peeking in on a rehearsal. And, in a way, it is just that. This conference may be only the first step for a playwright, who will continue to work on the play back home, with dreams of making it to Broadway. In that event, there will doubtless be reams of rewrites between the staged reading here at O'Neill and a full production in a Broadway theater.

This intimate "theater-in-the-raw" experience may take place in the red barn, known as the Rufus and Margo Rose Theater Barn, or in one of the other two indoor barns. Outside, at the Edith Oliver Theater, or the Instant Theater, as it is called, the stage is a small wooden platform backed up against a humongous copper beach tree, estimated to be at least 100 years old. Small bleachers in front and on each side are designed to hold up to 125 people.

Eugene O'Neill Theater Center

Address: 305 Great Neck Road, Waterford, CT 06385.
Telephone: (860) 443-5378 year-round Mon–Fri 9-5:30.
Website: www.oneilltheatercenter.org
Summer Ticket Info: (860) 443-1238.
Dates of Operation: Mid June through mid August.
Hours: Tue–Sun Performance days: noon–8. Non-show days: noon–6.
Admission: Members $15; Non-members $20; Special pricing for Cabaret perfomances.
Directions: Available on website.

Several years ago, I saw the Hallmark Hall of Fame televised movie *The Piano Lesson*, based on August Wilson's Pulitzer prize-winning play. I thought of how exciting it would have been to see the play when it was first performed here in 1986, or one of his many subsequent plays that went on to Broadway and then to win Pulitzers or Tony Awards.

The Theater Center has also expanded over the past forty years. The National Playwrights Conference was joined in 1978 by The National Music Theater Conference, where *Avenue Q* was first performed and subsequently voted the Best Musical of 2004. More recently on the scene are the Puppetry Conference, the Cabaret & Performance Conference, and The National Critics Institute.

We enjoy everything about this delightful experience: the performance, an unequaled summer alternative to formal theater, the casual and relaxed atmosphere, and the perfect picnic setting.

▶ The Picnic

P icnicking at the Eugene O'Neill Theater Center is as intimate as the theater experience, and with everything in close proximity, we feel very much a part of the pre-theater hubbub.

The sunken garden is designed especially for picnicking, or visitors may use the picnic tables on the back porch of the main house known as The Mansion. The porch appeals to us, with an expansive view of green lawn abutted by sea grass and sand leading to Long Island Sound. When we learn that the participants of the conference sometimes work on this porch, we wonder how they are able to get any work done with so mesmerizing a view. But later, as we watch the play, it is obvious that great work indeed is accomplished here.

During intermission, packaged snacks, along with beer, wine, and soda may be purchased at the Blue Genes Pub. Box suppers may also be available—inquire at the box office.

▶ What's In Our Picnic Basket?

Fresh pears and Brie

▶ Gazpacho

Crusty Baguettes

METRO BIS

928 Hopmeadow Street
Simsbury, Connecticut
860-651-1908

Gazpacho

3 large cucumbers
3 red onions
8 plum tomatoes
1 green pepper
3 large stalks celery
2 tablespoons salt
1 tablespoon pepper

2 tablespoons sugar
5-6 dashes Tabasco
1 tablespoon Worcestershire sauce
1-46 ounce can tomato juice or V-8
2 tablespoons lemon juice
1\2 bunch cilantro about 2 ounces
1 tablespoon cumin

- Cut the cucumber lengthwise and scoop out seeds with the tip of a teaspoon and reserve seeds. Then cut lengthwise into 1/4 inch strips. Stack the strips of 1/2 a cucumber and turn perpendicular to the knife and cut into 1/4 inch dices. Repeat with rest of cucumbers. Makes about 4 cups.

- Peel red onions and cut in half top to bottom. Pull 3 layers of the onion apart and slice into 1/4 inch slices. Then turn and cut into 1/4 inch dice. Repeat doing no more than 4 layers at a time. Makes about 3 cups.

- Cut plum tomatoes in half top to bottom and scoop out seeds and reserve. Cutting top to bottom slice into 1/4 inch slices. Then turn and cut into a 1/4 inch dice. Repeat with the rest of the tomatoes. Makes about 4 cups.

- Cut the top and bottom off the pepper and reserve. Cut the pepper away from the seeds into 4 leaves. Now slice each leaf into 1/4 inch slices. Then turn and cut into the same 1/4 inch dice. Makes about 1 cup.

- Wash the celery and trim off leaves and reserve. Cut stalks into 1/4 inch lengthwise strips. Stack strips and cut into a 1/4 inch dice. Makes about 1 cup.

- Put all the chopped vegetables into a 2-gallon plastic bucket and mix with the 2 tablespoons salt, 1 tablespoon black pepper, 2 tablespoons sugar, Tabasco and 1 tablespoon Worcestershire sauce and let sit for 10 minutes.

- Place the reserve cucumber seeds, tomato seeds, top and bottom of the pepper, and the celery leaves into the bowl of a food processor and puree for 1 minute.

- Add puree to vegetable mix.

- Pour 1 – 46 ounce of tomato juice or V-8 into the vegetables and add the lemon juice, chopped cilantro, and cumin and refrigerate for 1 hour.

- Taste and adjust seasonings with more lemon juice, salt and Tabasco.

- Serve in chilled bowls with sliced crusty baguette and garnish with cooked salad shrimp or avocado.

- Serves 8-10

Hartford

I invited some out-of-town friends on a mid-week walking tour of downtown Hartford, and thought that while I was sharing some favorite historical sights, we could also look for places to picnic in the middle of the city. What we discover is that thousands of office workers already know where to picnic. Everywhere we walk, people have claimed various nooks and crannies as their very own outdoor lunch spots: a bench for sitting, a spot of lawn for lounging, or a rock for leaning.

We begin at the **Old State House,** one of the oldest in the nation (1796). This National Historic Landmark was designed by Charles Bulfinch in the Federal style. First on the agenda is an audio tour that guides us through historic rooms, such as the Supreme Court and the magnificently restored city council and senate chambers. Next is a fascinating and stimulating exhibit that impressed me so much I went home and recommended it to everyone I know. *History is All Around Us* is a new 6,800 square foot interactive multi-media exhibit that tells the story of Hartford and the historical influence this city has had in our everyday lives during the last six centuries. Don't miss it.

Now, we climb a flight of stairs to see (of all things in this stately place) Joseph Steward's Museum of Curiosities. We are especially curious about the calf with two complete heads. It seems that Mr. Steward occupied space in the Old State House almost from its beginning, first painting portraits, then opening a Museum of Natural and Other Curiosities. Admission was 25 cents. The size and popularity of Mr. Steward's collection eventually required him to move to other quarters, but now, it seems only fitting that a re-creation of his original collection would come back to where it all started, the Old State House.

Hartford:

Old State House:
800 Main Street,
(860) 522-6766.
Website:
www.ctosh.org.
Hours: Tue–Fri 11–5;
Sat 10–5. Closed
Holidays.
Admission: Adults $6;
Seniors (65+), Students
with ID, and Youths
(6-17) $3; Children under
6 Free; Old State House
and CHS Museum
Members Free. First Sat
of every month from
10–1 Free.
Location: Corner of
Main Street and Central
Row. Building is handi-
capped accessible.
Directions and Parking:
Visit website for directions
from 84 East and West
and 91 North and South.
There are several parking
garages within a
comfortable walking
distance. Old State
House has arrangements
with Constitution Plaza
South Garage (Kinsley
Street), to validate visitor's
tickets for a flat rate of
$5. Check website for
directions to garage.

Before we leave, we visit the new Museum Store, chock-full of unique quality books and gifts, many of which are made here in Connecticut and other New England states. We like that.

Outside, picnic options are on a bench facing Statehouse Square or on the east lawn in front of the building. (Note that the front of the building faces the river—it's the back of the building that faces Main Street.) On days when a noontime concert is scheduled, claim one of the folding chairs lined up on the lawn. If the Farmer's Market is here (June through October on Monday, Wednesday, and Friday between 10-2) take advantage of the opportunity to purchase fresh Connecticut produce to supplement your picnic.

Next, we cross Market Street to climb the stairs (or the ramp on the left) to **Constitution Plaza**, named for the world's first written constitution drawn up in Hartford in 1639. This plaza has been described as an "urban park," even though there is hardly a blade of grass. Never mind, the folks pouring out of their offices at lunchtime head directly to their favorite stone benches near the fountain or the clock tower. While reading books or chatting with friends, they enjoy brown bag picnics. Today, as well as other days during the summer months, Riverfront Recapture has arranged for a musical group to perform here during lunchtime.

From Constitution Plaza, we head over to **Riverfront Plaza**, passing under the tall silver masts that mark the Phoenix Gateway. The plaza is a wonderful space for city-sponsored activities throughout the year. Today, folks are simply meandering or eating lunch at one of the park benches provided on the left of the walkway. A low, flowing stone wall runs the entire length of the walk on the right side, and provides another place to eat or perhaps to rest a guitar or other musical instrument case while entertaining visitors, impromptu style. At the end are nearly a hundred steps leading down to the river, or one may opt to use a combination of ramp and elevator to reach the riverbank. Here, landlubbers

Travelers Tower Tours:
1 Tower Square.
(860) 277-4208
For voice mail reservations, although reservations not necessary.
Hours: Mid-May through mid-Oct Mon–Fri 10:15–2:30. Closed Holidays.
Admission: Free.

Wadsworth Atheneum:
600 Main Street,
(860) 278-2670.
Website: www.wadsworthatheneum.org.
Hours: Wed–Fri 11–5; Sat–Sun 10–5; First Thurs 11–8. Closed Holidays.
Admission: Adults $10; Seniors (62+) $8; Students (13 + and College with ID) $5; Children (12 & under) free. 1st Thursday of every month from 5–8. $5 Pass for free admission to General Exhibits (2 adults & 2 children) can be obtained from CT public libraries.

Municipal Building:
550 Main Street.
Hours: Mon–Fri 8:30–4:30. Closed Holidays.

Bushnell Park Carousel:
(860) 232-6710.
Website: www.BushnellPark.org.
Hours: Early May to late Oct Tue–Sun 11–5.
Cost: $1.00 per ride.

picnic on stone benches or green grass while watching the ever-changing river activity. We discover that on certain days we can be part of that activity by boarding Hartford's newest riverboat, *Lady Katharine*, for a lunchtime cruise.

Leaving the south end of the Plaza (the left side of the Plaza when facing the street), cross Prospect Street and walk down one block to the glass rotunda on the right, the entrance to **Travelers Tower**. Take an elevator to the top (or rather to the 24th floor—70 steps complete the climb) and you may be singing, "On a Clear Day You Can See Forever." Back outside, picnic on round stone benches encompassing flower containers. Before we leave, I point out one of my favorite sculptures by Frances Wadsworth. The bronze "Safe Arrival" depicts a family who came to settle in Hartford in 1636 with Thomas Hooker.

Directly across Atheneum Square is the side entrance to **Wadsworth Atheneum Museum of Art**, the oldest public art museum in America. Founded in 1842 by Daniel Wadsworth (1771-1848), the permanent collection contains more than 45,000 works of art. Highlights include world-renowned collections of the Hudson River School landscapes, Old Master paintings, modernist masterpieces, and French and American impressionist paintings. Contemporary art, changing exhibits, special exhibitions, lectures, tours, performances, films, and family events keep the museum exciting and fun for everyone. The museum also houses a restaurant and a gift shop.

When leaving the museum, look across Prospect Street to note the beautiful 55,000 square-foot building constructed in 1920, former home of the Hartford Times newspaper. The building's facade was brought to Hartford from an old church in New York City and was the site of addresses by Presidents Truman, Eisenhower, Kennedy, and Johnson.

Continuing south, we come to **Burr Mall**, a memorial to honor Alfred E. Burr, owner and editor of the Hartford Times for sixty-one years. One can't miss Alexander Calder's commanding orange sculpture, known as "Stegosaurus," towering over the minipark while sharing a cool space with a pool and fountains, white marble slab benches, and shade trees.

If a cold drink is needed about now, there is a snack bar in the basement of the magnificent **Municipal Building** (1914), which is accessible from the side entrance that abuts Burr Mall. Once inside, you may be tempted to climb the circular marble staircase to the first floor to admire the marble and glass floor, mammoth columns, and fancy scrollwork surrounding the balcony.

We exit the other side of Burr Mall on Main Street, turn right, walk one block, and cross Main Street. Nestled between the Gold Building and the Center Church (The Reverend Thomas Hooker was the congregation's first minister) is the **Ancient Burying Ground**, Hartford's first public cemetery dating back to 1640. Many stones make for interesting reading, and others, flattened by design or by time, make perfect improvised lunch tables. As one graveyard devotee explains, "It's so peaceful and tranquil here with all the happy angels looking over you."

If cemeteries tend to leave you with a grim feeling in which to digest lunch, simply exit the cemetery on Gold Street. Directly in front is a different kind of stone, in fact, any one of thirty-six in the **Stone Field Sculpture** by Carl Andre. Some of the boulders may make fine leaning posts while munching a sandwich and thinking about whether or not you appreciate the sculptor's work of art.

After all the marble and stone, some greenery is needed and we continue down Gold Street. Thanks to The Reverend Horace Bushnell, a Congregational minister and civil leader, in 1854 Hartford's citizens became the first in the world to vote for the purchase of land for a public park. **Bushnell Park** features more than six hundred trees of 125 varieties, and is host to several outdoor concerts during summer months.

There are a number of ways to get across the busy street to the park, but the easiest is to turn left and cross Gold Street onto Lewis Street. Walking a few feet down Lewis, we cross at the light and walk straight into the park. When we stay on the path and walk to the other side of the park, we come to my favorite reason for visiting—the 1914 vintage **Bushnell Carousel**.

At least once each season, I sit sidesaddle on my favorite white horse with elaborate carvings of pink and blue flowers. When the Wurlitzer Band Organ begins its lively tune and we start moving, I imagine prancing across the green grass on my way to an adventure, just like Mary Poppins. What a ride!

Take note of the Civil War Memorial Arch, a brownstone monument to the 4,000 Hartford soldiers who served in the War Between the States.

To picnic in the park, either claim a table outside the carousel building or spread a cloth anywhere on the spacious grounds.

I'm estimating that the entire walk from beginning to end is about 1-1/2 miles. Happy city touring and picnicking!

> ### ▶ Note:
> The Adriaen's Landing Project is making headway. Both the Convention Center and attached Marriott Hotel are thriving, the Connecticut Science Center is expected to be completed soon, and the Front Street Development of residential and retail facilities is under construction. As I pause to watch the Science Center construction from Constitution Plaza and Riverfront Plaza, it reminds me of something worth repeating. At any point in time, the information in a tour book is subject to change. This chapter, for instance, will have obvious omissions about future activities in this area of the City.

What's In Our Picnic Basket?

Cheddar cheese slices

Mini bagels, sliced and buttered

Apple wedges (sprinkled with lemon
juice to prevent browning)

▸ **Loaded Oatmeal Cookies**

Loaded Oatmeal Cookies

Everyone in the Mann family has an insatiable sweet tooth, so I created an oatmeal cookie that is loaded with luscious, rich extras. My advice is to hide them in the bottom of your picnic basket until after lunch, as they have been known to disappear faster than you can say, "Dessert anyone?"

1 cup (2 sticks) butter, softened	2 teaspoons baking powder
1/2 cup granulated sugar	1 teaspoon baking soda
1 cup light brown sugar, packed	1/2 teaspoon salt
2 eggs	2 cups oatmeal
1 teaspoon vanilla	1 cup dried cranberries
2 cups all-purpose flour	1 cup white chocolate morsels
	1 cup coarsely chopped pecans

▸ Preheat oven to 350 degrees F.

▸ In mixing bowl, blend butter and both sugars with electric mixer. Add eggs, one at a time, beating well after each. Add vanilla and mix into batter. In another bowl, combine flour, baking powder, baking soda, and salt; add to creamed ingredients, mixing well. Add oatmeal, cranberries, chocolate morsels, and pecans to batter and blend.

▸ Drop dough by heaping tablespoon onto ungreased baking sheets.

▸ Bake for 10-12 minutes or until set and just barely golden.

▸ Leave in pan for 1-2 minutes; remove to rack to finish cooling. When cool, pack in covered container to keep fresh and soft.

▸ Yield: About 4 dozen.

New Haven

We find the area in and around the New Haven Green busy, exciting, and alive with options. Our first walking tour feels like a treasure hunt, as we seek out historical, cultural, and entertainment activities.

There is no problem finding a parking meter on Elm Street and walking one block to our first stop, **Info New Haven**, located on Chapel Street at the west corner of the Green. Here, we make inquiries and pick up maps and literature to help us plan our half-day adventure.

In 1638, when the Colony was first established, the founding fathers developed the nine squares city plan, giving New Haven the distinction of being the first planned city in America. The symmetry of the design was meant to provide a focal point for the city's religious, social, political, and educational development; it also makes it easy for visitors to find their way around. The middle square, where we are, is the Town Green.

First, we walk around the perimeter of the square, noting that each street has its own distinctive identity. Elm Street is home to the Library, Superior Court, and Yale Visitor's Center; Church Street finds City Hall, the Amistad Memorial next to City Hall, U.S. Courthouse, and Financial Center; Chapel Street contains shops and restaurants; and, College Street houses—you guessed it—the old Yale Campus.

Back in the interior of the Green, we admire the three churches sitting side by side on Temple Street, all built between 1812 and 1815. Each church has a unique history and shares architectural excellence in the styles of Gothic, Georgian, and Federalist.

New Haven:

Directions: From Hartford I-91 South, Exit 3, left onto Orange, right onto Chapel, right onto College (street parking available) or next right onto Elm (street parking available).

Info New Haven: Corner of Chapel St. & College St. (for maps & info). **Hours:** Mon–Thurs 10–9; Fri & Sat 10–10; Sun 12–5.

Greater New Haven Visitors Bureau: 169 Orange Street (203) 777-8550. **Website:** www.visitnewhaven.com (for free Visitor's Guide, Events Calendar, Area Maps, and other information, like a free downtown trolley.

Trinity Episcopal Church: (203) 624-3101. **Website:** www.trinitynewhaven.org. **Self-Guided Tours:** Mon–Wed 9–2; Thurs 9–6; Fri 11:30–1:30; Sat 9–1; Sun 7:30–3.

Trinity Episcopal Church is one of the first authentic Gothic buildings in America. The well-known Trinity Choir of Men and Boys, founded in 1885, performs at most Sunday 11:00 a.m. services.

Center Church on the Green, founded in 1638, has been called a Georgian masterpiece and is the fourth Center Church to be built on the Green. This church is known for its Tiffany stained-glass window above the alter and a historic crypt in the church basement.

United Congregational Church—This Federalist style design was taken from London's St. Martin-in-the-Fields. Renovations have restored the interior, although the shallow dome, ceiling ornament, and chandelier are original.

Since we have time to tour just one church, we choose the Center Church because we are intrigued with the idea of a church being built over a portion of the original Colonial burial ground. During a tour of the crypt, the guide points out the gravestones of several dignitaries and shares their connection with New Haven. The rest of the burial ground is located in back of the church, although there are no markers. Apparently, no one knows how many graves there are or the exact dates. Although records date from 1687 to 1812, it is suspected that earlier graves do exist.

After a picnic break, we decide to walk to two museums located on Chapel Street, just one block from the Town Green. (Oops, first it's time to feed the hungry parking meter again.)

Yale University Art Gallery is the oldest university art museum in the United States. Founded in 1832 with Colonel John Trumbull's gift of his paintings of the American Revolution, this impressive exhibit takes up an entire wall of the Trumbull Gallery. A larger-than-life 1792 painting of General George Washington at The Battle of Trenton is the focal point. Detailed

Center Church on the Green: (203) 787-0121. **Tours:** Apr–Oct Thurs and Sat 11–1 or by appointment.

United Congregational Church: (203) 624-0698 or (203) 787-4195.

Yale University Art Gallery: 1111 Chapel Street, (203) 432-0600. **Website:** www.artgallery.yale.edu **Hours:** Tue–Sat 10–5; Sun 12–5. Closed major holidays.

Yale Center for British Art: 1080 Chapel Street, (203) 432-2800. **Website:** www.yale.edu/ycba. **Hours:** Tue–Sat 10–5; Sun 12–5. Closed major holidays.

and realistic paintings of the Revolutionary War and small portraits of significant leaders during that period surround it.

Yale Center for British Art is in possession of the most comprehensive collection of British art outside the United Kingdom. Here, we are drawn to a temporary exhibit called Whistler: The Naval Review. This proof set of the twelve etchings completed and presented to Queen Victoria during her Jubilee in 1887, are signed in pencil with Whistler's signature butterfly.

Both museums are sure to entice us back during the year for films, concerts, lectures, and tours, in addition to the art exhibits. By the way, everything including admission is free!

Gift shops and other delights are in abundance on Chapel Street. During our walk back, we are only too happy to browse in some of them, all in the name of research, of course. We also stop at a confectioner's shop for ice cream since we did not include dessert in our picnic basket.

Yale Campus Tour is not on today's agenda; however, Yale is a significant part of New Haven that defines not only the historical and cultural fabric, but the tempo of the entire City. I had the opportunity to take a tour a few years ago and was impressed by the history of this institution and the beauty of its campus. Tours are offered twice daily. Visitors can sign up at the Yale Visitor's Center on Elm Street, or simply stop in and pick up a map for an independent tour.

Although our focus is on the Green and nearby museums, this is not to imply that everything of interest is contained within the nine squares city plan. Attractions such as Peabody Museum, the Long Wharf Theatre, the Coliseum, Broadway with its bustling shops, fine ethnic restaurants, and historical attractions lie just outside this area, justifiably attracting large numbers of visitors to this City.

I hope daytrippers will enjoy this bird's eye view of New Haven as much as we did. Now that we have our bearings, other attractions are tempting us to venture outside the box, or in this case, the square!

▶ **FYI**:
A parking lot on York Street, around the corner from the Yale Center for British Art, may be an alternative to parking at metered spaces on nearby streets. This would allow more time at the museums without being interrupted to feed the meters. Just be aware that there are a lot of one-way streets in this area, so do consider beginning at the Visitor's Center, as suggested.

▶ The Picnic

As we search for the best place to picnic on the town green, we note that Temple Street divides the green into two distinct areas.

One half of the green is a large, open area. This is where summer concerts and other planned activities take place, such as symphonies, jazz concerts, festivals, parades, or one of many holiday happenings. Today, dozens of bicycles are casually lined up with their riders astride, and we suspect that a race is about to start.

The other side of Temple Street, where the churches are located, functions as a park. A dad throws a ball to his son, while Mom and a younger sibling look on. Later, a couple plays Frisbee. On this mild Saturday in late May visitors have the luxury of choosing from benches in a sunny location or nestled among shade trees.

First, we walk back to the car to feed the meter, retrieve our picnic basket, and the material from the Information Center. Then, we select a bench with a view of a large flowering chestnut tree where we have lunch and read about all the upcoming events scheduled for this city.

▶ Curried Chicken with Cashews on a croissant

Cherry tomatoes

Curried Chicken with Cashews

(Courtesy of Holly McCarthy)

The melding of pungent curry and sweet raisins is what makes this chicken salad special. And the cashew topping is the crème de la crème. We enjoy this particular chicken salad on a croissant, but it's also good served on a bed of lettuce.

2 cups cooked chicken, finely diced
1/2 cup finely diced celery
1/4 cup raisins
1/4 cup orange juice
1/2 cup mayonnaise
1/2 teaspoon curry powder

Pepper to taste
1 teaspoon fresh lemon juice
4 large croissants
Lettuce or spinach leaves
1/2 cup unsalted cashews, chopped

▶ Bring raisins and orange juice to a slow boil to plump raisins. Remove raisins from juice and cool. Place chicken, celery, and raisins in a salad bowl.

▶ In small bowl, combine mayonnaise, curry powder, pepper, and lemon juice. Add to chicken mixture and blend well. Chill.

▶ Cut croissants in half lengthwise. Place lettuce leaves on bottom of croissant. Top with chicken mixture. Sprinkle with cashews.

▶ Yield: 4 sandwiches

 Travel Tip   If you are planning to eat within a couple of hours after preparing sandwiches, they should keep well. Otherwise, consider packing chicken mixture, rolls, lettuce, and cashews separately and assembling right before eating.

Fall Fun
& Foliage

Elm Knoll Farm
Somers

W hat does the month of October mean to children? Halloween, hayrides, and haunted houses of course, not to mention pumpkins and the latest craze, the corn maze.

A good place to find all this and more is at Elm Knoll Farm. And the "more" comes each year when the owners add new displays to entice not only children, but entire families. There are so many things to see and do that maps are sometimes passed out at the entrance, where the price of admission includes all activities.

We start at the petting zoo, which contains the usual farm animals, as well as a few animals that surprise us. First, we are drawn to the squealing piglets that are raising a ruckus because mother pig is resting rather than nursing. Next, we are amused by the antics of a wallaroo playing with one of the workers. The rest of the residents are in various stages of typical animal behavior, including prairie dogs doing what they do best wherever they reside—burrowing.

Next, we are off for a wagon ride to the corn maze. The maze is huge and we have the option of exiting halfway through, which some of our party take advantage of. But, not to worry, there is no chance of getting lost in this kid-friendly maze, and amusing signs along the path keep it interesting. When we are ready to go back, the hay wagon picks us up for a pleasant ride through the woods to the pumpkin patch.

Pumpkins, pumpkins, everywhere, not only in the pumpkin patch, but also doubling as heads on all the characters in the enchanting Mother Goose Land. The almost life-size creations, complete with props and the appropriate nursery rhymes, catch

Elm Knoll Farm

Address: Pinney Road, Somers, CT 06071.
Telephone: (860) 749-9944.
Website: www.elmknollfarm.com.
Open: Late Sept–Oct (exact dates vary from year to year.)
Hours: Everyday 10–5.
Admission: Weekdays $5; W/E & Holidays $7; Age 2 and under Free. Special group rates. Haunted rides additional.
Directions: Interstate 91, exit 47E, east on Route 190 to Somers, right onto Maple Street (first light in Somers), left at fork, follow signs.

Note: Check out the popular Haunted Hay Rides on Saturday and Sunday evenings in October.

my full attention. I am only halfway through the display when the younger members of the group skip off to investigate the tepee and wigwam made of corn stalks. Just as I catch up, they are already heading for Noah's Ark.

Finally, our group comes together for a walk through the haunted barn—there is safety in numbers, you know. Our imaginative youngsters almost tremble with the anticipation of ghosts and goblins popping up out of black spaces and they are not disappointed.

Outside again, we zigzag across the grounds to see if we missed any displays and to revisit our favorites. As we meander around on this beautiful fall day, we are entertained by a live band performing in the music shell, the sounds mingling with the melody of a happy community.

▶ The Picnic

There is more than enough space for some serious picnicking at this farm. An open front structure directly across from the refreshment stand holds several picnic tables and is perfect for a large crowd or if the weather is less than ideal. Today, we choose one of the tables scattered about the grounds, not only to enjoy the crisp fall weather, but to be in the midst of all the fun.

Homemade or Deli Meat Balls

Assorted Cheeses

Small Rolls for Accompaniment
  or Sandwich

Side Salad

▶ **Apple Harvest Cake**

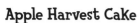

Apple Harvest Cake

I can't remember where I found this recipe, or how it was altered through the years, only that it has always been a family favorite.

5 apples
6 tablespoons sugar
2 teaspoons cinnamon

4 eggs
2-1/3 cups sugar
1 cup vegetable oil
1/3 cup orange juice
2 teaspoons vanilla
3 cups flour
1-1/2 teaspoons baking soda
1-1/2 teaspoons baking powder
1/2 teaspoon salt

▶ Peel and pare apples. Cut into thin slices. Combine sugar and cinnamon and mix into apples. Put to one side.

▶ Preheat oven to 350 degrees F.

▶ With electric mixer, blend eggs, sugar, oil, orange juice, and vanilla. In separate bowl, combine flour, baking soda, baking powder, and salt. Add to liquid ingredients and blend with mixer. Continue mixing at medium speed until thick and lemon colored.

▶ Grease and flour bundt pan. Batter and apples are added to pan in layers, 3 for batter and 2 for apples. Begin and end with batter.

▶ Bake for 1-1/2 hours. Place on rack to cool for 10 minutes. Turn pan upside down on cooling rack, allowing cake to drop out of pan.

Football Tailgating Party
New Haven-Yale/East Hartford-UConn

The idea of a chapter on football tailgating intrigued me for a couple of reasons. First, it would be a new experience, and second, it appeared to be a good fit for my goal of diverse chapters. The usual format of activity and picnic does not work however, because by its very definition, tailgating is picnicking. So, in this chapter, the picnic itself is the activity.

As I was seeking answers as to what it is about tailgating that appeals to so many, I discovered the website of Joe Cahn, the Commissioner of Tailgating. He says, "Tailgating is the last great American neighborhood, the tailgating neighborhood, where no one locks their doors, everyone is happy to see you and all are together sharing fun, food and football."

With his cat "and navigator" Sophie, a pot of Jambalaya, and a 40-foot motor coach, Joe has traveled thousands of miles to football stadiums across the country with the intent of making new friends and sampling tailgating fare.

Take a look at Joe's website to see amazing tailgating stories from around the country—from those who set up large tents with chandeliers hanging from the tops, to male students dressed in their finest coats and ties. And pig roasts! Speaking of tailgating food, wait until you see the variety of recipes.

I was intrigued with this website and wanted to find out more, so I contacted Joe. He graciously agreed to a telephone interview.

I asked Joe how he got elected commissioner. "In 1996 I wanted to see if I could live in a motor home. In one year, I visited every stadium in the NFL and fell in love with tailgating. At first I thought I should be 'King of Tailgating' but kings can be

Yale Bowl, New Haven

Yale Athletic Department: (203) 432-4747. **Website:** www.yale.edu/athletic/facility/bowl. **Directions:** See website.

Rentschler Field, East Hartford

UConn Football office: (860) 486-2718. **Website:** www.rentschlerfield.com (for tailgating rules); www.uconnhuskies.com (for tickets). **Directions:** See website.

Joe Cahn's website: www.tailgating.com.

overthrown, whereas commissioners are for life. In 1997, when I was at NFL Headquarters, I had the microphone, so I named myself Commissioner. No one objected."

Does he agree with me that tailgating is the ultimate picnic? He does, adding that Yale claims to have started tailgating back in the early nineteen hundreds. Yale-Harvard was the big event then, as it is today, and many of the fans and alumni worked in New York. There was no stadium (the Yale Bowl opened on November 21, 1914) and no food to be had at the games, so fans started packing picnics.

I saw from his posted schedule that Joe visited Rentschler Field in 2004. His notes say that "tailgating on the runway of the gauntlet (as it is now known) is one of the fascinating sights in tailgating. On the opposite side of the stadium is a grassy area with just what every tailgater wants—space and grass instead of asphalt." He also mentions the enthusiasm of the fans and the variety of food cooking on the grills. During the interview, we chat about how amazing it is to stroll along the wide runway leading up to the stadium with tailgaters parked and partying on either side.

What advice does this seasoned tailgater have for the new tailgater, someone who may be thinking about trying it for the first time?

"Arrive early—two to four hours early—pack a small lunch, bring a chair or two, then walk around, talk to people, get ideas, get enchanted and amazed at what you see."

I asked about equipment. Joe said, "Anything and everything goes, even a rickety card table with cheese whiz." I agree that you do not need any special equipment. If you have a folding table, great, but a ground cloth will work. If you do not have a portable gas grill, bring cold food in a cooler. If you like tailgating and want to invest in some equipment, there are a lot of choices. But, don't buy before you get an idea of what will work best for your style of tailgating. This means, as Joe says, talking to and visiting with people. Joe likens a tailgating parking lot to a kitchen. Everyone is invited in. He calls it the best cooking school in the country.

Joe is not only a worthy Commissioner of Tailgating, but a great ambassador. It is his love for and enthusiasm of this event that makes him the perfect spokesperson.

Although I do not bring the experience of Joe Cahn to these pages, I can offer some information to fellow novice tailgaters about what to expect based on my journal entries from the Yale and UConn stadium parking lots. This is by no means a complete picture, but merely a snapshot based on a two-hour period of meandering at each destination. Each person's impression of tailgating will vary considerably depending on many factors, beginning with the parking area you are ushered into based on arrival time, and your neighbors. But part of the fun of tailgating is having a new, different experience each time. Here is mine.

YALE: It is raining lightly on the morning of the Yale-Princeton football game. Still, from the moment I pull into the parking lot, I sense the beginnings of a party atmosphere, with tailgaters in various stages of setting up. One woman excitedly tells me this is her first tailgating party, and as she is already perched on a tailgate, it looks like she is ready to begin. She invites me back later when they start cooking. I'm not sure what time this will be, but when she tells me she is not going to the game, I'm guessing that once the party does get underway, it will continue throughout the afternoon.

I walk between the rows of vehicles—mostly cars and SUVs, some trucks, and one RV, where the cook is passing food out to guests through the open door. I am curious about a line of U-Hauls I spot in the distance and when I make my way to them, I find the Yale student territory. It is at once obvious that they are the most ingenious and enthusiastic tailgating group here. Strolling up and down what I dub "tailgaters' campus," I cannot resist peering unabashedly into the open backs of the U-Hauls looking for decorating styles. The first is completely empty, allowing space for people to stand in out of the rain. The next one has about a dozen folding chairs, all empty at this time, and I can't help but smile at the set-up—classroom style. The third contains a rather lumpy, stuffed sofa. A setting for every mood!

Now, onto more important research – the cooking apparatus. Large gas tanks are hooked up to a variety of charcoal cookers. All shapes and sizes are in evidence, the biggest one made from a large barrel. The cook tells me he used 2 1/2 bags of charcoal and the bottom is barely covered. The two small burgers look lonely as they sizzle in the middle of the grill. Portable generators provide power to a variety of electrical appliances, from burners and bean pots to griddles and coffee pots.

I am curious as to what is brewing, stewing, frying, or broiling in the various receptacles, but I am not bold enough to interrupt the party to inquire. What I can actually see are merely the expected dogs and burgers. Sandwich fixings are being lifted out of coolers and mountains of munchables are laid out on tailgates and tables, some with cloths, one with a flower centerpiece. More than a few glasses of wine are in evidence, plus lots and lots of beer.

Soon, I am damp and hungry, so I venture over to a tent sponsored by a radio station, with a sign inviting fans to come inside for free food. I put away my notepad and pen and try to look like a fan. Sure enough, I am offered a hot dog and soda which are going fast, and before I even finish eating, a donut company is taking down their stand. There is plenty of fun for kids as well. Inside a nearby tent there are a variety of table games and outside, an artificial climbing wall.

Other sponsored tents are sighted in the distance and I begin to comprehend the size of this place. It occurs to me that I have not covered even one-quarter of the grounds, but since it is nearing game time I do not venture back out in the rain to continue my research.

UCONN: From young babies to seasoned elders, every age group is represented at this tailgate party before the UConn-Liberty game. Many folks I talk with have season tickets and have been tailgating for years, even bringing their babies with them so they won't miss a game. There is no lack of enthusiasm and team spirit. The Huskies logo is affixed to everything from tee shirts, hats, and mugs to canopy tents.

There are more regulations here, presumably due to the fact that neighborhoods surround the stadium as well as the parking lot. For example, no charcoal grills are allowed. So, there are portable gas grills. The other major difference is that tailgating is confined to before games. Once the game begins, no one is allowed to stay in the parking lot, although there is a small number that do. There is no post-game tailgating either, but realistically, it takes over an hour to clear the parking lot.

I want to figure out the typical tailgater's schedule, so I pay particular attention to timing. Here is what I find:

Four hours before game time—gates open. Folks lining up at this hour are eager to get the best parking spaces, those closest to the stadium. Two hours before game time—vehicles are still pouring into the fields abutting the stadium. One and one-half hours before game time—the scent of food is strong, not only from a variety of food and spices on the grills, but from greasy takeout. Cold sandwich fixings are a popular choice for lunch, accompanied by the usual snack foods. One-half hour before game time—folks begin cleaning up, chairs, tables, and grills are collapsed, folded, and packed in trunks, trash is loaded into bags, and car doors locked. Everyone is in high spirits as they make their way towards the stadium. Game time—a scattering of stragglers are still heading to the stadium, and a few folks are getting comfortable in chairs behind their cars and tuning their radios to the game station, or chatting with companions.

One hour after game time—I finished my research almost one hour ago and want to go home. I am still looking for my car. That "Tips from Tailgaters" suggestion on Joe's website, the one about tying a helium-filled balloon to the antenna—it's a good one.

▶ What's In Our Picnic Basket?

MORNING GAME:

▶ **Stuffed French Toast**

    Turkey Sausage

    Home Fries

▶ **Hot Spiced Cider**

AFTERNOON GAME:

Snacks

▶ **Joe's Jambalaya**

    Rolls

    Sweets

Stuffed Tailgate French Toast

(Courtesy of Barbara Rodegher)

    I had it on good authority that Barbara was both a tailgate aficionado and a good cook. When I called her to ask for a recipe, this one immediately appealed to me because it is different from the usual tailgate recipes. I tried it out in my kitchen during the summer and loved it. Now I'm all set for football season. It does require a Cut and Seal gizmo, a round press that crimps two slices of bread together to make a pocket while cutting off the crust. They may be called something different but are available in kitchen shops.

2 loaves sliced bread (I found that
    the really soft bread seals the best)
4-5 eggs, depending on size
1/2 cup milk

ADULT FILLING :

3 apples, chopped

3 bananas, chopped

1/2 cup brown sugar

1/4 cup dark rum

1/2 cup slivered almonds

KID FILLING :

1 pint strawberries

1 pint blueberries

1/2 cup sugar

- DAY BEFORE: Place all adult filling ingredients, except almonds, in a saucepan and simmer over medium heat just until the apples begin to soften. If filling appears too juicy, add 1/2 teaspoon flour and cook until filling has thickened. Add nuts. Refrigerate.

- Combine all kid filling ingredients and refrigerate.

- MORNING OF THE EVENT: To make pockets, spread bread slices on counter. Place one tablespoon filling in the middle of each slice. Cover with second slice and press with the Cut and Seal utensil. You should have a nice round pocket with the sides tightly pinched to keep filling inside.

- Place pockets in a sturdy container to transport to destination.

- In a portable container, mix eggs and milk.

- AT THE EVENT: Preheat griddle. Dunk pockets into the egg mixture. Cook on first side until lightly brown, then turn over and brown the other side.

- Serve with choice of toppings. Powdered sugar, syrup, or whipped cream are favorites. Try a few chocolate chips on top of the whipped cream.

- Servings: 8–12

▶ Joe's Jambalaya

Joe Cahn, Commissioner of Tailgating, says "This is my favorite recipe because you can put just about anything in it. If it walks, crawls, swims or flies, it can be thrown into Jambalaya. Everything goes into one pot so clean-up's a breeze."

(12–15 servings)

1/4 cup vegetable oil
1 1/2 lbs. boneless skinless chicken
   breasts, cut into 1 inch pieces
salt and ground black pepper
1 1/2 lbs. sausage cut
   in 1/4-inch slices
4 cups chopped onions
2 cups chopped celery
2 cups chopped green bell pepper

5 cups chicken stock or water
   flavored with chicken bouillon
1 tbs. minced garlic
4 cups long grain rice
2 tbsp. Kitchen Bouquet
   (browning agent)
2 tbsp. seasoning salt
2 cups chopped green onions

- Season chicken with salt and pepper; brown in hot oil in 8 quart Dutch oven or stockpot over medium-high heat.
- Add sausage; cook 5-to-7 minutes.
- Remove chicken and sausage from pan; set aside.
- Add onions, celery, green peppers and garlic; cook, stirring 7-10 minutes or until vegetables begin to wilt.
- Stir in chicken stock, reserved chicken and sausage, seasoning salt and Kitchen Bouquet. Bring to a boil.
- Add rice and return to a boil.
- Cover and reduce heat to simmer.
- Cook 10 minutes; remove cover and quickly turn rice from top to bottom completely.
- Replace cover and cook 15 to 20 minutes or until liquid is absorbed and rice is tender.
- Stir in green onions.

For brown jambalaya, add 1 heaping tbsp. brown sugar to hot oil and caramelize, or make a roux, or use Kitchen Bouquet. For red jambalaya, add approximately 1/4 cup paprika or use 1/2 stock and 1/2 tomato juice or V-8 for your liquid. For seafood jambalaya, add cooked seafood when rice is cooked.

If using an electric stove, reduce cooking time by 3-4 minutes.

Four Tips:
- Use 1 cup of rice for every 2 cups of vegetables (onion, celery, bell pepper)
- Use 1 1/4 cups of liquid for every 1 cup of uncooked rice
- 1 cup of uncooked rice will make 3 cups of cooked rice, season accordingly.
- Cook jambalaya for a total of 25 to 30 minutes, stirring well after 10 minutes.

► **Hot Spiced Cider**

Just the thing on a chilly, fall day.

1. Pour 4 cups apple cider into a saucepan.
2. Add 2 cinnamon sticks and a teaspoon of whole cloves.
3. Bring to just below boiling point.
4. Remove from heat.
5. Strain.

OPTIONAL : Stir in 1/2 cup ginger brandy.

► Pour into thermos to keep warm. A metal thermos will keep warm for four hours; a plastic thermos will keep warm for up to two hours.

► When serving, pour into cups and add one-half of a fresh orange slice.

► Yield: 32 ounces.

Kent Falls State Park & Cornwall Covered Bridge
Kent & West Cornwall

A t peak fall foliage (around mid-October in Connecticut) it is our custom to join the throngs of other tourists hop-scotching across Litchfield County in search of the autumn beauty, which is as fleeting as an ice sculpture in spring. There is a rhythm here that permeates the entire area, perhaps having to do with the seasons that change so rapidly, from the lazy yawns of summer to the brisk shouts of autumn.

Two of our favorite destinations are just seven miles apart and we visit them on the same day. Kent Falls is a series of waterfalls that begin in the town of Warren on a mountain stream known as Falls Brook. Here, the falls plunge approximately seventy feet in a dramatic cascade, then descend in a series of lesser falls and cascades to the valley, where they enter the Housatonic River some 200 feet below.

Kent Falls is an easy place to get to and welcomes visitors immediately with a parking lot that is right off the main road. Pedestrians enter the park through a covered bridge, an authentic reproduction built in 1974, then cross the meadow to the foot of the falls. Anxious to ease the car riders' kinks, we immediately begin our 1/4 mile climb to the top. Although fairly steep, vantage points along the way allow us to pause and view the majestic falls from different angles. Soon, we realize we've worked up an appetite, so it's back to the meadow for an autumn picnic, enhanced by the combination of our short hike, the brisk air and the rushing falls.

Nourished by food, exercise, and nature's beauty, it is time to head to the Cornwall Covered Bridge in West Cornwall. We drive through the narrow 173-foot long bridge, which has been

Kent Falls State Park

Address: 159 Macedonia Brook Road, Kent, CT 06757.
Telephone: (860) 927-3238; or State Parks (866) 287-2757.
Website: www.ct.gov/dep/site. Click Outdoor Recreation; click State Parks & Forests; click Find a Park.
Hours: 8am–sunset.
Parking Fees: W/E & Holidays from mid May through the end of Oct: CT residents $7; non-residents $10.
Location: Route 7 approximately 3 miles south of intersection with Route 45 and approximately 4.5 miles north of the village of Kent.

Cornwall Covered Bridge

Location: West Cornwall, Route 128. From Kent Falls, continue north on Route 7 to Route 128. The distance from Kent Falls to the Covered Bridge is about 7 miles.

in continuous service since 1864, park the car on the other side, and walk through the bridge and back again, peeking out the window openings on each side for postcard views of the Housatonic River. Soon, we are part of the camera-toting crowd that is snapping shutters faster than you can say "cheese." Our lens is pointed at pink wildflowers amidst red and gold foliage on the banks of the river with the magnificent red bridge in the background. And, if we stick around long enough, we may be able to add windbreaker-clad paddlers in red kayaks or marine blue canoes to the picture.

If time allows, poke around the small town of Cornwall. There are interesting shops and, if desired, restaurants to supplement the picnic fare brought from home.

Kent Falls State Park.
Picnic tables and pedestal grills are lined up next to the small brook that runs along the entire length of the meadow. On the other side of the meadow are a few more tables. The choices range from a table close to the falls, or one farther away with more privacy.

We've planned a versatile menu that can be casually eaten either in one "sitting" or over a period of time. If the weather is chilly, we move around to stay warm while the grill is heating up, poking around the rocks near the base of the falls or having a lively game of Frisbee in the middle of the meadow.

Cornwall Covered Bridge

There are a couple of picnic tables and some benches on the banks of the Housatonic. Or, if weather permits, spread a blanket on the best spot to view the river activity.

Sometimes, our lunch becomes a progressive meal. We eat the main course at Kent Falls and the dessert at the Cornwall Covered Bridge, allowing us to stretch out the picnicking along with the day.

Assorted Chips & Fruit

Grilled Hot Dogs & Hamburgers

▶ **Carousel Chili**

Macaroni & Vegetable Salad

Dessert Bars

Carousel Chili

(Courtesy of Deborah Dierman)

A friend gave me this recipe a few years ago, when another friend and I were hosting our joint birthday party at the Bushnell Carousel. We rented a hot dog cart and served this chili as an accompaniment to the dogs. It was a big hit, and I immediately renamed the recipe (sorry, Deb). Of course, it is just as delicious served in a bowl with a bread accompaniment and a sprinkling of parmesan cheese. And, as may be expected, it tastes even better the next day.

The recipe is pretty simple. The only thing to emphasize is that the kidney beans must be the baked variety to give the chili that extra sweet flavor. (You may not find them in the usual canned bean aisle and may have to ask a store clerk for *baked* beans.)

For all you knock-your-socks-off chili fans out there, you might find yourself pulling all the stoppers out of your spices in order to dump them into the chili pot, because this recipe is only mildly spicy, just the way I like it. Whatever degree of spicy/hot you prefer is up to you, but you won't go wrong when you start out with this basic recipe.

Carousel Chili

2 tablespoons olive oil

2 medium onions, sliced thin

2 green peppers, sliced

1 pound lean ground beef

4 cloves garlic, minced

2 cans (28-ounce) Italian
plum tomatoes

2 cans (16-ounce) kidney
beans, baked

2-3 tablespoons tomato paste
(to thicken)

2 tablespoons chili powder

1 teaspoon paprika

salt and pepper to taste.

▸ Heat olive oil in nonstick skillet on medium heat and add onions and peppers. Sauté for 7 minutes or until onion is translucent. Remove to Dutch oven. Add ground beef to skillet. Season with a dash of chili powder, salt and pepper. Cook until no longer pink. Drain fat and add to Dutch oven. Turn down heat and add garlic to same skillet, adding a little more olive oil if needed. Sauté for 1 minute, stirring constantly. Combine with peppers, onions, and beef.

▸ Add the tomatoes, breaking up with spoon. Stir in beans, tomato paste, chili powder, paprika, salt and pepper. Cover and simmer for 50 minutes, stirring occasionally.

▸ Servings: 8–10 bowls or unlimited hot dog garnish.

Mohawk State Forest
Cornwall

I n this chapter, I describe the Activity and the Picnic at the same time as I cannot seem to separate them. They just go together, like fall and foliage.

I remember years ago when our Sundays were reserved for family excursions. Sometimes, the focus was on the destination, like a daylong picnic at our favorite lake. Other times, the focus was on the drive itself. The destination became whatever we happened upon—an ice cream shop, a farm stand, or a local park in which to meander about while snapping photographs.

Mohawk State Forest is both a drive and a destination, and is especially suitable for mid-October when Connecticut's crayola mountains are at their most beautiful.

The drive up the 1,683-foot mountain, just under 4 miles, is lovely. It does not compare, however, with the view waiting for us at the top—an awe-inspiring panorama of Mount Greylock to the north, Heublein Tower and Avon Mountain to the East, Redding Ridge and Naugatuck Forest to the south, and the Catskill Mountains to the West.

A roundabout for parking, three picnic tables, and a wooden lookout tower complete the picture. I'm guessing the tower to be about 40-50 feet high, and the 35 steps are both steep and narrow. Still, it appeals to the more active folks in our group, who crave both the exercise and the reward of yet another perspective of the majestic mountains. A scenic drive climaxed by an awesome destination with perfect picnicking facilities. Who says you can't have it all!

Mohawk State Forest

Address: 20 Mohawk Mountain Road, Goshen, CT 06756.
Telephone: (860) 491-3620.
Website: www.ct.gov/dep/site. Click Outdoor Recreation; click State Parks & Forests; click Find a Park.
Hours: 8 am–sunset.
Directions: From the center of Litchfield, go north on Route 63 to the rotary in Goshen Center, then Route 4 west approximately 4 miles to the entrance on the left. Consult website for more complete directions.

If there had been small children in our group, we probably would have driven back down the mountain for our picnic rather than worrying about the danger of youngsters wandering too close to the steep slope. During the drive up, we noticed several pull-off areas alongside the road, complete with tables and either upright charcoal grills or stone fire pits.

This Sunday or any-other-day-of-the-week drive is also suitable for folks whose physical movement may be restricted. Not only is the overlook wheelchair accessible, but both the scenery and the picnic can be enjoyed from the car.

▶ **FYI:**

This state forest also contains a Black Spruce Bog, which is extremely uncommon in Connecticut. It features the last stages of a process that began about ten thousand years ago, and has been described as an "outstanding living museum of the State's natural history." Look for a sign on the drive up the mountain leading to a parking area with more information, plus a walking trail to the Bog. Hiking, pond and stream fishing, and skiing are also on the list of activities for this destination.

▶ What's In Our Picnic Basket?

Hot Soup (In Thermos)
▶ Spicy Cheddar Crackers
Sweets
Cold Cider

Spicy Cheddar Crackers
(Courtesy of Holly McCarthy)

This cracker log can be mixed and stored in the refrigerator for up to two weeks. Slice and bake whenever fresh crackers are needed to perk up a picnic. My favorite is to pair the baked crackers with fresh apple slices and serve as an appetizer with a glass of wine or sparkling soda. These crackers also work well as an accompaniment to soup or salad.

1/2 pound cheddar cheese,
   finely grated
1/4 pound butter, softened
1-1/2 cups flour, sifted
1/2 teaspoon dry mustard
1/4 teaspoon salt
1/8 teaspoon cayenne

- Preheat oven to 350 degrees F.

- In large mixing bowl, mix all ingredients thoroughly with hands. On floured surface, shape the dough into two logs, each 6-inches long and 1-1/2-inches round. Roll in wax paper and refrigerate for at least one-half hour.

- Using a sharp knife, slice dough into 1/8-inch rounds. Place on ungreased cookie sheet. Bake for 12-14 minutes or until golden brown. Cool completely on a rack before storing.

- Yield: approximately 8 dozen.

 **Travel Tip** Store in airtight plastic container. To transport, place scrunched up plastic wrap on top of crackers before adding lid. There will be less chance of breakage if crackers are secure.

Air Line Rail Trail
A CT Greenway, State Linear Park & Trail
East Hampton, Colchester & Hebron

I t is late summer when we mount our bikes at Cranberry Bog in East Hampton, eagerly anticipating a scenic trail with a number of diverse enhancements. In fact, there are visual surprises around almost every bend of the ten-mile stone dust trail, from stone crops suddenly looming before us to the meadowland's display of green ferns interspersed with white, purple, and gold wildflowers. We hug the middle of the trail, when on either side there appear sheer drops to a valley, the depth of which we can only imagine. Later, we stop to admire the Salmon River State Forest's dense woodland, stretching out to a distance we cannot measure. A river, brook, creek and marsh round out the natural surroundings, while a bridge and two viaducts provide historic interest.

An added bonus is the opportunity to enjoy natural areas that abut the main trail—a hike in the Salmon River State Forest in Colchester, the Grayville Falls Park in Hebron, and the Raymond Brook Marsh, a wildlife habitat, also in Hebron. Or, we can take a detour off the Air Line Trail for further explorations. A four-mile link to the Colchester Railroad Trail will bring us close to historic Colchester Center, and the town of East Hampton can be reached by leaving the trail for a stretch of on-street biking.

All this information, and the location of seven parking areas along the trail, is listed in a map provided by the Parks and Recreation Departments in the three towns.

The Air Line Rail Trail is the site of the original New York & Boston Railroad. The dream of a train traveling between New York and Boston was conceived in the mid-1800s by a group of investors and engineers. They envisioned the Air Line route from

Air Line Trail:

Obtain guide and map at: The Parks and Recreation Department or the Town Clerk's Office at the **Municipal Building:** Town of East Hampton, 20 East High Street, (860) 267-6020. Town of Colchester, 127 Norwich Avenue (860) 537-7297. Town of Hebron, 15 Gilead Street (860) 228-5911 Ext. 2. **Website:** http://pages. cthome.net/mbartel/ ARRabout.htm

the idea that "if a line had been drawn through the air" between New York and Boston, it would be a faster and better route. The first problem was bridging the three-quarter mile wide Connecticut River in the Middletown area and the numerous trap rock ridges in various other sections of the State.

Even before solutions to these issues were found, there was a series of misfortunes in the form of financial scandals, excessive costs, and bankruptcy before eventual reorganization. During this time, the original New York & Boston Railroad changed hands and names several times. Determination prevailed, however, and with costs that far exceeded original estimates and a path significantly different from the first design, the dream became a reality. It took twenty-four years.

Ironically, it is this very success that led to the railroad's demise. As freight increased, the additional weight began to restrict travel over the steep grades, numerous curves, and viaducts and much of the trail ultimately had to be discontinued. The year was 1937, and several years later, the railroad went into bankruptcy.

The state acquired the rights in the 1980s and the Department of Environmental Protection proposed the rehabilitation of the rail bed as a 50-mile plus multipurpose trail and linear state park. A regional effort by the Towns of East Hampton, Colchester, and Hebron resulted in the completion of this section of the trail, now suitable for joggers, walkers (with or without leashed dogs), bicyclists, wheelchairs, horseback riders, and cross-country skiers.

While writing this chapter, I began to envision what this area might look like during other seasons: autumn, when nature proudly flaunts her foliage; winter, with majestic black branches abutting a snow covered trail, green pines standing at attention in the distance; spring, when colorful borders of scented wildflowers and new forest growth embroider the landscape.

Amongst all the colors of nature, our first glimpse of bright blue in the distance is almost startling. Could it be? Sure enough, it really is a couple of picnic tables with attached benches—one almost hidden behind foliage and another sitting in the sun at the edge of the trail.

I guess it shouldn't be surprising that the town employees and volunteers who constructed this trail thought to provide their visitors with the ultimate picnicking opportunity. In addition to the tables, a number of benches invite us to stop periodically to rest, quench our thirst, and gaze into the beautiful distance.

▶ What's In Our Picnic Basket?

Trail Mix (Dried Fruits & Nuts)

Sandwich: Hard Cheese on Buttered
Pumpernickel with Grainy Mustard

▶ **Vegan Peanut Butter-
Chocolate Chip Cookies**

After I tasted this wheat-free and sugar-free cookie at a tea shop in Canton, I asked for the caterer's name and telephone number. Immediately after Erin sent the recipe to me to include in my book she received a job offer in Hawaii and said Aloha. I was told the ingredients can be found in just about any natural foods store.

Erin's Amazing Vegan Peanut Butter-Chocolate Chip Cookies
(Recipe courtesy of Erin Schuh)

3 cups white spelt flour
1 teaspoon baking soda
1/2 teaspoon sea salt
1/2 cup vegan margarine
　(Earth Balance is a good one)
2-1/2 cups natural peanut butter
　(the kind that's just peanuts)

1/2 cup plain soymilk
3/4 cup pure maple syrup
2 teaspoons vanilla
1 bag vegan grain-sweetened
　chocolate chips
　(Sunspire makes good ones)

▶ Mix all ingredients together along with a few heaping scoops of love (the most important ingredient)... Drop whatever size spoonfuls suit your fancy onto parchment-lined or lightly greased cookie sheets. Bake for 10-20 minutes (depending on cookie size) at 350 degrees. Serve warm from the oven with tall glasses of soymilk! Take a moment to breathe in the sweet yummy scent and thank the infinite universe for all of life's blessings... Enjoy with a good friend... Share this divine cookie goodness and love with the world! Have a glorious day!

▶ Yield: 18 medium–large cookies

Erin can be reached at VerdantCircle@yahoo.com

Devil's Hopyard State Park
East Haddam

If you are in the mood to hike through woods hued with hemlocks, fish for trout in a rushing brook, or be mesmerized by a cascading waterfall, head for Devil's Hopyard. Have a rousing volleyball game, let your children wade in the brook, string a hammock between obliging trees, relax and listen to a ball game, or practice your drumming. Visitors here not only come to enjoy typical park activities, but are comfortable enough to bring their own activities as well.

For serious hikers, there is a posted map of the trails across from the parking area at the first entrance to the park, or download beforehand from the website. Today, we continue driving to the entrance for the "Picnic Area." After parking, we walk through a covered bridge to cross the river, then turn left on the orange trail and follow it up the hill to the top, catching glimpses of the falls through the foliage. Later, we remembered a better view from the other side of the falls: take the road to the left of the picnic area (walk around the log barrier) and continue uphill.

Devil's Hopyard became a state park in 1919 and much of the history seems to revolve around the origin of its name. The numerous tales of devils and potholes, and of hops grown nearby, have surely been altered and embellished through the years due to the colorful imagination of visitors. Still, we are somewhat disappointed that we can neither verify nor add to the folklore. Remarkably, there is not one strange figure in our midst, nor any hops for that matter. None that we can see anyway!

Devil's Hopyard State Park

Address: 366 Hopyard Road, East Haddam, CT 06423.
Telephone: (860) 873-8566; or State Parks (866) 287-2757.
Website: www.ct.gov/dep/site. Click Outdoor Recreation; click State Parks & Forests; click Find a Park.
Hours: 8 am–sunset.
Directions: From CT Route 9, take Exit 7, left at end of exit ramp onto Route 154 North, right at first traffic light and follow signs. Drive past the first park entrance and turn in at the second entrance with a sign stating "Picnic Area, Hiking, Fishing."

O f all the tables situated in the picnic grove, those next to the river seem to draw the most occupants because of the peaceful, yet energizing environment. We also like the fact that the tables are spaced far enough apart to afford privacy, if one desires, although we see some men move two tables together to accommodate their large group.

This site is ideal for a full day, or at least a half-day, of fun and relaxation, including a picnic with all our favorite foods. Indulgence comes to mind, especially when we see a man wheeling over a large gas grill for what promises to be an elaborate picnic. But, not to worry, there are the usual pedestal charcoal grills scattered about, however, as is the case with many state parks the grates tend to be rusty, so either bring your own grate or tinfoil to cover the existing ones.

Today, however, is but a pleasant interlude in an otherwise busy day, so we have packed a simple lunch of rolls, sandwich fixings, and various accompaniments, and carry the small cooler and picnic basket to the foot of Chapman Falls. Walk up the road until you see a path with wooden steps. Head downhill just a few steps and take an immediate left along a narrow dirt path until you come to a clearing at the foot of the falls. Note that although this path is short, it is somewhat rugged. Therefore it is only suggested for the surefooted.

After taking a few minutes to look over our options we spread an ample picnic cloth on a choice rock. It is not the smoothest or the most level rock, but it is the largest, and we can sit on either end using the middle as a table, of sorts. And the view is perfect!

▶ **FYI:**
A large picnic pavilion located opposite the main picnic area is available for rental.

Appetizer

▶ Halibut en Papillote with Pesto

Grilled Vegetables

Crusty Bread

Fresh Peach Shortcake

Halibut en Papillote with Pesto

(By Chef Richard Moriarty)

At the Center for Culinary Arts, students learn that steaming is a terrific way to prepare nutritious meals quickly. En papillote (awn-poppy-yote) is a cooking method where the food is steamed in its own juices. Parchment paper or aluminum foil is used to wrap the food in a tight package, providing a neat, quick efficient cooking medium. And here's the best part. If you use tinfoil to create your papillotes you can cook them outside on the grill.

These bundles of flavor can be prepared in advance and cooked quickly at service time. Foods that are appropriate for steaming are vegetables, fish and shellfish. Halibut with pesto en papillote is an easy fix that still looks elegant, even presented in aluminum foil.

Serves 2

1 Pound fresh halibut steak

Salt and pepper, to taste

1 Oz. dry white wine

4 Tbs. pesto

Tinfoil, one sheet about 14 inches long

▸ Place the halibut in the center of the foil and season lightly with salt and pepper. Drizzle the wine over the fish. Spread the pesto over the top of the fish in an even layer. Fold the long sides of the foil over the fish and seal by crimping the edges together. Then twist one end into a tight seal and bend it upward into a thin handle. Repeat with the other end. Refrigerate until ready to cook.

▸ Preheat the grill to hot. Place the tin foil papillote on the grill and cook until done, about 10-12 minutes. Unseal the foil and serve at once.

Basil Pesto
Makes about 2 1/2 cups

6 Cloves garlic, peeled
1 Cup Fresh basil leaves, washed
1 Cup Fresh curly parsley, washed
3/4 Cup Pine nuts or walnuts, rough chopped
1 Cup freshly grated Parmesan cheese.
3/4 Cup Olive oil
Salt and pepper, To Taste

▸ Place the garlic in the work bowl of a food processor fitted with the metal blade. Process until the garlic is minced. Add the basil and parsley leaves and pulse until minced. Add the nuts and pulse until well chopped, but not fine. Add the cheese and pulse until just mixed. With the processor running, add the oil quickly and process until just mixed. Adjust seasoning with salt and pepper.

▸ This pesto freezes well, and can be used in many different recipes. Here are some suggestions: as a sauce for hot or cold pasta, spread generously inside grilled cheese sandwiches, as a garnish for soups, mixed with regular mayonnaise for a great sandwich spread.

Heublein Tower at Talcott Mountain State Park
Simsbury

It's a one and one-quarter mile climb up from the parking area at the entrance of Talcott Mountain State Park to the highest point of the mountain, 875 feet. At the top is the most distinguished feature of the park, the 165-foot high Heublein Tower. Now, more climbing, exactly 120 steps to the Tower's observation room at the top (we didn't read this, we counted), well worth the effort for the thrill of the dramatic 360-degree view of four states.

Gilbert F. Heublein built the Tower in 1914 and the attached fieldstone house in 1926. Heublein, president of the liquor and food company by the same name, resided in this summer retreat with his family for approximately thirty years. Printed literature in glass cases in the former living room recounts the fascinating history of the Heublein family as well as this versatile area, from the 1770s to the present time. It explains the structural and scientific reasons why this Tower manages to survive when the previous three towers on this site did not. There are also maps showing additional hiking on a section of the Metacomet Trail.

The Friends of Heublein Tower have taken an active role in the restoration and upkeep of this state park. Both the dining room and Gilbert's bedroom have been renovated for visitor viewing, and the current project, the observation room in the Tower is expected to be completed soon. Just as the living room is used to present the personal history of the Heublein family and how they lived, the observation room will tell the corporate story. The artifacts that the Heublein Corporation donated before its move from Hartford will add many more dimensions to this interesting man, Gilbert Heublein.

Heublein Tower at Talcott Mountain State Park

Address: Route 185, Bloomfield, CT 06002. **Telephone:** Park Manager (860) 242-1158. **Website:** www.ct.gov/dep/site. Click Outdoor Recreation; click State Parks & Forests; click Find a Park. **Hours:** Park: Daily 8 am–sunset; Tower: Memorial Day–Labor Day Thurs–Sun 10–5; Labor Day–Oct 31 daily 10–5. **Location:** Parking area and entrance to Talcott Mountain State Park is on Route 185, seven miles west of Hartford, diagonally opposite the entrance to Penwood State Park. Access to the Heublein Tower is by foot trail.

Back outside, the stunning flora and fauna surrounding the home, plus the stone masonry and other added touches reflect the Heubleins' love of nature and their surroundings. There is also evidence of the stone fireplace that was built for roasting sheep on an electronically-powered spit, a favorite entertainment for guests.

We marvel at the 85-foot barbecue pit built for the occasion of a visit by (then General) Dwight D. Eisenhower. The gathering at Heublein Tower included many notables, for it was here that the future President was asked to run for office.

It is hard to convey the level of difficulty of the hike, since the terrain feels quite different under every hiker's shoes. All ages seem to do well at their own pace, except occasionally young toddlers will do what mine used to do, reach out their arms and say "up." Parts of the trail are rather rocky and the beginning section is somewhat steep.

During my first hike on this trail, my shoes easily strolled past a father and a mother at the beginning of the trail. Well, okay, the father was carrying a toddler on his shoulders and the mother, a baby in a harness. But, these same shoes also passed folks who were not carrying anything. I must admit, however, that halfway up the mountain my initially enthusiastic shoes went from a brisk walk to a slow stroll to a panting pause, as I watched every person I previously passed now leave me in the dust.

I soon realized that it matters not how long the climb takes but that the activity provides as much joy and stimulation as the destination. This is easily accomplished by pausing to savor the view from the impressive overlooks along the way. A favorite is the Hang Glider Overlook, the largest clearing on the edge of the cliff. I still remember a serendipitous occasion when we happened upon hang gliders using this spot as a launching pad. During every visit since then we hope to see them again, but, as yet, have not.

Every season has its own rewards, both along the trail and at the top of the mountain. Autumn brings the most visitors, drawn to the colorful foliage, while late spring and summer is distinguished by the beauty of the plants and flowers. And, of course, the tower is open during these seasons. I haven't trekked up the mountain during winter yet, but have heard about folks who make an annual pilgrimage here on New Year's Day. Sounds like fun!

▶ The Picnic

Picnicking. This is the complete description of what I previously read about the facilities at Heublein Tower. Therefore, the grand and versatile picnic areas were a delightful surprise during the first visit, and they continue to amaze me each and every time. Part of it, I think, is seeing the grills standing like sentries near the picnic tables. They are all cold. The irony is that there are such splendid picnic facilities in an area that is somewhat difficult to get to by oneself, never mind while lugging the fixings of a picnic worthy of such accommodations.

Until I can figure out an easy way to carry a cooler, picnic basket, and charcoal up the mountain, I will be content with an easy backpack picnic. With several distinctly different picnic areas, wherever we decide to spread our checkered cloth will be just right for the mood of our party.

Picnic tables set in a grassy clearing near the tower are protected from the wind and the atmosphere is peaceful and serene. Only a few feet away, and perfect if you hunger for more sweeping vistas, are tables closer to the cliff, where you can feast on both your lunch and the view, a la carte.

A stone pavilion just beyond the barbecue pit provides a distinctively different atmosphere for a picnic. Ideal for a larger group because of its spaciousness and privacy, it would be equally welcome as a temporary retreat during a sudden change in our New England weather.

Finally, for folks who don't need a table and want to forge their own picnic place, just look around. The grassy areas and large rocks seem to be inviting picnickers to simply plunk down and enjoy the mountaintop.

> ▶ **Note:**
> There are no trash receptacles at this site so picnickers should be prepared to carry everything back home.

Favorite Munchies

▶ Surprise Roll Sandwich

Fresh Apples

Surprise Roll Sandwich

(Courtesy of Terry Bernard)

This is a fun sandwich—first, because the hot dog roll is a change from the usual sandwich bread or roll, and also because of the surprise filling within the filling. Try different varieties of meats and cheeses to wrap around the coleslaw.

    1 package (8) hot dog rolls
    3/4-1 pound sliced ham, not too thin
    1/2 pound Swiss cheese
    coleslaw

- ▶ If desired, spread butter or mayo on the inside of the roll.

- ▶ On one or two slices of ham, place one slice of cheese. Spread one-half of the cheese with coleslaw* and roll up starting with the long side. Place in hot dog roll.

- ▶ Makes 8 sandwiches

- * Coleslaw recipe (see Recipe Index) or purchase deli coleslaw along with the sandwich fixings.

Travel Tip For a backpack picnic, pack in cooler while driving to the destination. Then transfer to an insulated sandwich bag that will fit in your backpack. Or, wrap well and put in plastic bag with a small ice pack.

The White Memorial Conservation Center
Litchfield

White Memorial, the state's largest nature center and wildlife sanctuary (4,000 acres), is surely one of Connecticut's best four-season activity and picnic areas.

Thirty-five miles of scenic trails beckon hikers, bikers, and horseback riders, while equally satisfying but less intense activities are plentiful, such as: Observe the resident birds from Observation Towers on Apple Hill, traverse the wooden boardwalk through wetlands, and experience the one-quarter mile "Trail of The Senses" to observe the natural environment through the use of sixteen interpretive plaques. To get the most pleasure out of your visit, consider purchasing a Trail Map at the Museum. (The cost is $3.00.)

Winter finds cross-country skiers and snowshoers using the same thirty-five miles of trails, and in summer nearby Bantam Lake, the largest natural lake in Connecticut, draws visitors to its bathing, fishing, and boating facilities.

As we tour the Nature Museum, located in the former home of Alain and May White, we learn that the Center exists because of the White's generosity. By 1912, they had acquired 4,000 acres of land for conservation purposes. They established the Memorial Foundation to preserve land for future generations to enjoy, whether on foot, on horseback, or on the water.

This museum is extraordinary. Dioramas, with a background of photographic murals, depict many diverse habitats, and animal mounts strategically placed amidst nature's bounty allow us to take a unique journey through this wildlife refuge. A special taxidermy exhibit tells us how the mounts were made. Every

The White Memorial Conservation Center

Address: 80 Whitehall Road, P.O. Box 368, Litchfield, CT 06759.
Telephone: (860) 567-0857.
Website: www.whitememorialcc.org.
Hours:
Trails: Always open. Museum: Mon–Sat 9–5; Sun 12–5. Closed major holidays.
Cost: Museum: Adults $5; Children (6–12) $2.50; Age 5 & under free.
Location: Located off Route 202 between Litchfield and Bantam, approximately 2 miles west of Litchfield on Whitehall Road.

nook and cranny has been filled with captivating exhibits, many interactive and all fun. The live animals and a Nature Store are also favorite places to visit inside the museum.

Special environmental and educational programs are also offered during the year. On this 4th Saturday in September, it is "Family Nature Day." Ten minutes after we pick up a schedule of events, we are paddling a canoe on The Bantam River. Later, we stop to listen to a banjo and fiddle duet before heading to Ongley Pond for an adult program on "Pond Life Discovery." Nets and strainers are provided for catching tadpoles, small fish, and insects along the bank, which are then examined and enhanced with a microscope. Later, as we learn about the three kinds of plant life found here, someone spots a beaver across the pond chewing on a tree branch that he has dragged away from the edge of the shore.

Additional activities to choose from today are numerous: for adults, exhibits and demonstrations on a variety of topics; for children, stories, games, and a fishing derby; and tours and nature walks for everyone. All in one day and all for a nominal fee.

▶ The Picnic

Picnicking is not only encouraged at White Memorial, it seems to be part of the curriculum. Numerous picnic tables are strategically placed in all key areas—near the museum, the pond, and along the trails.

After the lecture ends at Ongley Pond, we claim a table nearby so we can continue watching the beaver. Or, maybe watching the beaver chew so ravenously makes us hungry! Either way, the table is also close to the lot where our car is parked, so we easily retrieve and enjoy our own lunch.

▶ What's In Our Picnic Basket?

Tortilla Chips & Salsa

▶ Wild Rice and Ham Salad

Pumpkin or Zucchini Bread

Watermelon Slices

Wild Rice & Ham Salad

This is one of my favorite luncheon salads. The ingredients complement each other perfectly. Deli ham is fine, but I prefer to have the butcher cut one thick piece so I can cut it into bite-size chunks. Sometimes I use brown raisins because they always seem to be on hand, however the golden raisins have a more subtle flavor, providing just the right amount of sweetness to offset the onions. You can be flexible about most of the ingredients—just don't skip the pecans. They make as much difference as the frosting on a cake.

2 cups cooked wild brown rice

1/2 pound lean ham, cut into bite
    size chunks

1/2 cup golden raisins, soaked in hot
    water for 20 minutes and drained

1/4 cup thinly sliced scallions

salt & pepper to taste

1/3 cup olive oil

1/4 cup red wine vinegar

1/2 cup pecan halves

- In small shallow pan spread pecan halves in a single layer. Bake in 350-degree F. preheated oven until toasted—approximately 5 minutes. Watch closely. Cool. (I personally like smaller pieces so I cut them in half again.)
- In large bowl, stir together rice, ham, raisins, and scallions. Add salt and pepper.
- In small bowl, whisk oil and vinegar together until well blended. Slowly pour over rice and ham mixture until the salad contains the amount that suits you. (I almost never use the entire amount.) Toss.
- Serve at room temperature or chilled. Just before serving, garnish with pecans. Serve on lettuce leaves.
- Serves 4-6

Travel Tip Refrigerate salad overnight, or at least two hours before packing in cooler.

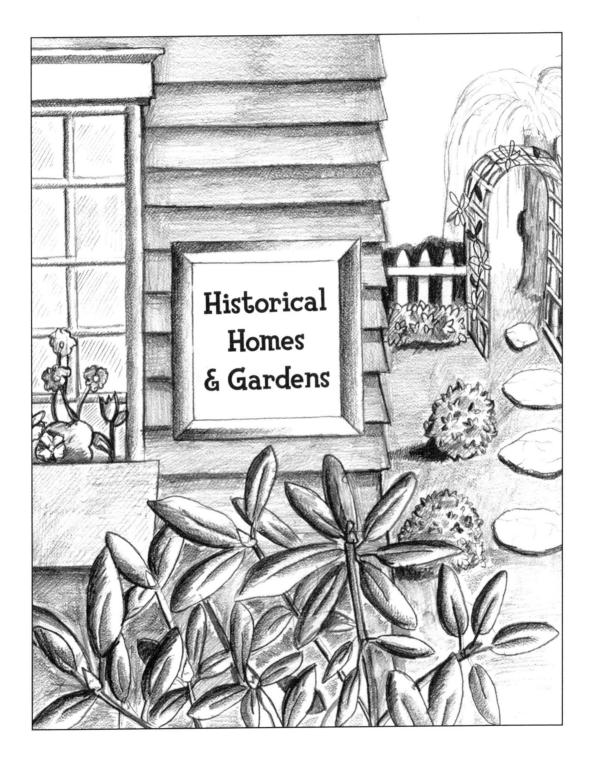

Historical
Homes
& Gardens

Boothe Memorial Park & Museum
Stratford

Meet David and Stephen Boothe, successful farmers and businessmen: "We were both born in the 1860s in the 1820s family homestead and lived our whole lives here. We wrote President Roosevelt in 1943 to verify the claim that it was the oldest homestead in America. He never wrote back so we voted Republican after that."

The brothers were proud of their homestead, built on the foundation of the family's original c. 1663 home. Their legacy includes many of the original furnishings, as well as old letters, bills, receipts, family books, and Bibles. The Boothes never threw anything away; in fact, their greatest enjoyment seemed to be in collecting, especially what they considered important artifacts from America's past. The most unusual might be the one-thousand used horseshoes.

When the antiques became so numerous that the brothers ran out of space, they solved the problem by simply buying or building museums. It appears that at some point the accumulation of buildings became as much fun as the collections themselves.

The Clocktower Museum was the first, erected in 1913 to celebrate 250 years on the homestead. The clock with Westminster Chimes and five massive bells engraved with the family's genealogy is purported to be the oldest working Howard clock in the world. Previously situated above the ceiling, the clockworks were recently lowered to eye level, and a trench was dug for the pendulum. Now, visitors have a close-up view of this impressive clock, one of the highlights of the tour. But, there are plenty of other highlights as well.

Boothe Memorial Park & Museum

Address: Main Street Putney, P.O. Box 902, Stratford, CT 06615.
Telephone: (203) 381-2046.
Hours: Park grounds open year-round 9–5.
Museum Tours: June 1 through beg. of Oct (call for exact dates) Tue–Fri 11–1; Sat–Sun 1-4.
Admission: Donations.
Directions: From Merritt Parkway, exit 53, proceed south on Route 110 to Main Street Putney which forks to the right, head south one quarter of a mile to the park on left. From I-95 westbound, exit 38 (Merritt Parkway), continue to exit 53 and follow directions above.

Two of the buildings are especially unique. The brothers called the Redwood Building, built from California redwood shipped through the Panama Canal, a "one-of-a-kind showpiece." Wait until you see why!

Another unusual structure is the Blacksmith Shop, built with forty-four sides and corners, a blatant attempt to outdo Henry Ford's four-sided Blacksmith Shop in Michigan. But, even though the buildings awe us, it is still the collections inside that leave us wondering—how could two men amass such an assortment of objects?

Even the décor in the homestead reveals the brothers whimsical nature, we think, as we chuckle over the jigsaw-puzzle tile floors. And, oh yes, the house holds collections as well, like baskets that fill an entire room.

The grounds are well maintained, and we enjoy walking in the All American Rose Selections accredited garden. The Friends of Boothe created a wedding garden in the same area, centered with an antique fountain.

A "miniature Sturbridge Village," I thought out loud during the tour, but the difference, I was told, is that when school groups visit they actually get to weave the rugs and make the apple cider, providing an active rather than a passive tour.

The greatest pleasure for the Boothes seemed to be sharing their artifacts with others. To this day, they are still drawing people to their homestead, thanks to both the Town of Stratford and the Friends of Boothe. Their combined efforts have made it possible to keep the buildings and grounds open to visitors, not only for tours, but also for meetings, festivals, and even weddings in the Putney Chapel.

David and Stephen Boothe would have been pleased.

▶ The Picnic

It is an added bonus that the Boothe Memorial Park & Museum does not overlook the value and delight of a picnic area in which to pause and refresh during a day's outing. Picnic tables are situated at the back of the property in a large, inviting setting of green lawn and huge shade trees. For the youngsters in your party, there is also a small playground close by.

A newer area for picnicking and fun, but with a greater concentration on the playground, can be found down the hill from the parking lot.

▸ What's In Our Picnic Basket?

Wheat Crackers with Pate
or Cheese Spread

Favorite Sandwich

▸ **Waldorf Deluxe Salad**

Waldorf Deluxe Salad

(Courtesy of Holly McCarthy)

We took a basic Waldorf salad recipe, added a zippy new dressing, and the result is our own Waldorf Deluxe. Our preference is to serve it either as a side with grilled meat or fish, or as a first course.

1/2 cup raisins

2 cups diced apples

1 tablespoon fresh lemon juice

1/2 cup diced celery

1/2 cup chopped walnuts, divided

Soften raisins in hot water for 20 minutes; drain and cool. Toss apples with lemon juice. Add celery, raisins, and one-half of the walnuts. Cover and refrigerate. Serve with Deluxe Dressing, topped with balance of walnuts.

Deluxe Dressing

1/2 cup sour cream

1 tablespoon mayonnaise

1 tablespoon frozen orange juice
  concentrate, thawed

1/4 cup finely chopped apples of choice

1 tablespoon finely chopped celery

▸ Combine all ingredients and mix well. Refrigerate at least one hour to let flavors blend.

▸ Serves 4-6

Travel Tip Pack salad, dressing, and the remaining 1/4 cup walnuts in separate containers in cooler. When ready to serve, fold dressing into Waldof Deluxe. Top with walnuts.

Florence Griswold Museum
Old Lyme

In the late nineteenth century, when Florence Griswold was having a difficult time keeping up her family home, she turned it into a boarding house. Soon after, a prominent landscape artist named Henry Ward Ranger visited and thought the location was ideal. This was the beginning of "America's first and most famous summer art colony." From the start, Miss Florence endeared herself to her guests with her kindness and generosity. Perhaps because of the environment she created for the artists, American Impressionism soon became synonymous with Florence Griswold and the Lyme Art Colony.

During a tour of the Greek Revival home built in 1817, we find the stories of this particular place in time and the artists who memorialized Old Lyme captivating. Particularly interesting are the paintings that decorate some of the doors and walls. Many of the artists, unknown at the time, painted in return for room and board or as a thank you to Miss Florence. I also envision, however, the close-knit group of artists simply having fun with these unusual canvases. My favorite is *The Fox Chase*, Henry R. Poore's painted panel over the dining room fireplace. Twenty-four fellow artists are pictured in unique and amusing poses, suggesting a warm camaraderie among the members of the Art Colony.

Just a few of the noteworthy paintings hanging in the house are Childe Hassam's *Church at Old Lyme*, William Howe's *Florence Griswold House by Moonlight*, and William Chadwick's well-known portrait of Florence Griswold, *On The Porch*.

The Museum, erected in the summer of 2002, invites visitors to view changing exhibitions of American art dating from the eighteenth through the early twentieth centuries. This museum

Florence Griswold Museum

Address: 96 Lyme Street, Old Lyme, CT 06371.
Telephone: (860) 434-5542.
Website: www.flogris.org.
Hours: Tue–Sat 10–5; Sun 1–5. Closed major holidays.
Admission: Adults $8; Seniors & Students $7; Children (6-12) $4; Under 6 free.
Directions: Interstate 95 to exit 70; follow signs.

has the distinction of owning one of America's leading collections of Impressionism, with major works by many artists who are featured in the house and the largest collection of Willard L. Metcalf paintings in the world.

One of my favorite Metcalf paintings is *May Night*. The story is that he first offered this painting to Miss Florence as a gift, but she refused it, sensing that one day it would be recognized as a great painting. It turned out that *May Night* was indeed instrumental to Metcalf's career as an artist.

After being exposed to all the fine paintings in the museum, many of which were created right outside its doors, you may be inspired to start painting yourself. Don't wait until you get home and the daily routine brushes the thought away before you can even get to the art store for fresh paints. If it happens to be a Sunday between mid-April and mid-October, you can start immediately.

First, take a quick look at William Chadwick's original studio building for another dose of inspiration. Then stop by the Hartman Education Center, which offers seminars and workshops. Here, you will be given a complimentary canvas, paints, brushes, and a palette to borrow. You don't even have to worry about your Sunday best, as old shirts are on loan as well. The landscape for your future masterpiece is just steps away, perhaps down by The Lieutenant River or Miss Florence's garden.

▶ **FYI**:
Upcoming exhibits, lectures and programs for every-one are described in an Events Calendar that will be mailed out upon request.

▶ The Picnic

O utside, the Lieutenant River draws us to its banks while the willows and sycamores motion to us to sit and be fanned by the gentle breeze. We are curious about a Split Leaf European Beech tree near the Garden Terrace, first examining what looks like a mysterious figure outlined in its trunk, then standing under the expansive canopy of foliage for another interesting view. Eventually, we determine the best spot on the lawn and spread our cloth to enjoy a peaceful picnic lunch. It just might be the exact spot where George H. Bogert painted *September Evening – Lieutenant River.*

▶ What's In Our Picnic Basket?

Cold Leftover Meat Loaf

▶ Blue Broccoli

Pumpernickel Party Rounds

Fresh Berries with

Vanilla Yogurt

Blue Broccoli

I enjoyed a similar salad sold by a market near my home for years. When they went out of business, I missed it so much there was nothing left to do but attempt to re-create it. My version has the same great flavor but a slightly looser sauce, which seems to enhance the broccoli.

1-1/2 lbs. broccoli	1 teaspoon lemon juice
1/4 cup red onion, thinly sliced rings	1/4 cup bleu cheese
1/4 cup sour cream	1/4 cup finely chopped walnuts,
1/4 cup mayonnaise	if desired

▶ Rinse broccoli and cut off stems leaving only the florets. Cook in microwave on high for 2-4 minutes, or in saucepan with a little water just until fork tender. Don't overcook. Rinse thoroughly in cold water to halt cooking and retain the bright green color. Drain well.

▶ Add onion. Mix sour cream, mayonnaise, and lemon juice together and add to broccoli. Fold in bleu cheese and walnuts. Chill.

▶ Serves 4-6

Travel Tip Refrigerate salad overnight, or at least two hours before packing in cooler.

Gillette Castle State Park
East Haddam

From 1899 to 1929, Hartford native William Gillette brought Sir Arthur Conan Doyle's character of Sherlock Holmes, the master detective, straight from the pages of books and onto the Broadway stage. Both the actor and the character became famous and, one could argue, somewhat synonymous.

In *The Adventures of Sherlock Holmes*, "Case of Identity," Sherlock said, "It has long been an axiom of mine that the little things are infinitely the most important." And, interestingly, Gillette himself placed great importance on "the little things." When he built this retirement home in 1914, he not only designed and directed the entire structure of the medieval-style castle, but also every amazing detail, both inside and out. Gillette's love of gadgets shows up in places like elaborately-designed latches for the forty-seven hand-carved doors, doorstops, and railway-inspired light switches.

During the entire tour, we get to peer through Sherlock's proverbial looking glass to discover surprises about both the castle and the owner's fun-loving antics, like a trick bar and the mirrors Gillette used to spy on his guests. In *The Adventures of Sherlock Holmes*, "Scandal in Bohemia," Sherlock said, "You see but you do not observe."

First, our guide points out highlights of the immense living room we are standing in and the atrium beyond, with the pond where Gillette kept his pet frogs, Mike and Lena. There are also anecdotes aplenty about Sir Henry and his other beloved cats. We are then invited to wander about this room on our own, as well as the rest of the house. Although the tour is self-guided, know-ledgeable attendants are close by to answer questions.

Gillette Castle State Park

Address: 67 River Road, East Haddam, CT 06423.
Telephone: (860) 526-2336.
Website: www.ct.gov/dep/site. Click Outdoor Recreation; click State Parks & Forests; click Quick Links.
Hours: Park: Year-round 8 am–sunset; Castle: Memorial Day W/E to Columbus Day 10–4:30.
Cost: Adults $5; Children (6-12) $2; Age 5 & under free.
Directions: From I-91, Exit 22 (9 south) to Exit 7 for bridge crossing of the Connecticut River. Follow Route 82E and park signs. From I-95 N or S, Exit 69 to Route 9N to Exit 7. For the Chester-Hadlyme Ferry, Exit 6, follow Route 148 and park signs. (The ferry operates from spring through fall.)

We especially enjoy Gillette's rather small but cozy bedroom with hidden closets, and the guest room where Helen Hayes stayed. In the impressive study are Gillette's original desk and shelves of books in the exact position that he left them. And a curious miniature door! In *The Adventures of Sherlock Holmes*, "Through the Magic Door," Sherlock said, "It is a good thing to start life with a small number of really good books that are your very own."

Standing on the garden patio later, it is easy to understand why Gillette became entranced with this hilltop, part of a series of hills known as the Seven Sisters. The panoramic view of the Connecticut River and the surrounding countryside is breathtaking, especially during autumn. Whichever season you visit, take time to enjoy some of the seven miles of well-maintained walking trails at this state park.

After the tour, we stop back at the Welcome Center to look at mementos and photographs of Aunt Polly, Gillette's beloved houseboat, and learn about Ozaki, the Japanese cabin boy who later became his trusted valet. But, the real treat is the display of the recently refurbished electric engine from Gillette's miniature railroad. I had always heard how he delighted in taking guests on a three-mile ride through the forestland and along the ridges of his property. There is no need to wonder who had the most fun on these adventures. From 1919 until his death in 1937, Gillette was the consummate king of his castle, and it is obvious that he enjoyed every minute of his reign.

There is a building with both inside and patio dining where you can buy refreshments. Expect the typical hot dogs, hamburgers, and snacks. Since this is a picnic trip, however, read on for two outstanding picnic options.

The first is next to a large pond to the immediate left after entering the park. On this day in mid-summer, it is covered almost entirely by variegated shades of pink, fuchsia, and white water lilies, and on closer inspection we see a frog hopping from one green lily pad to another. Really! Just beyond, dozens of picnic tables are nestled in the park's lush forestland, along with some freestanding grills. If you are planning to cook, this is the place, as there are no grills at the second picnic option.

Grand Central Station is just steps away from the castle. Originally built to accommodate Gillette's miniature train, this elaborate stone-covered structure now contains several picnic tables. The partially open sides provide for both a pleasant view and a welcoming breeze on this summer day.

▶ Tortellini Salad
Cold Cooked Sausage
Italian Bread
Chocolate Chip Cookies

Tortellini Salad

I have been enjoying this recipe for many years, and although I try other tortellini recipes from time to time, this is still my favorite.

20-ounce package mixed
  cheese tortellini
4 plum tomatoes, diced
1/2 red onion, chopped
1/3 cup Romano cheese
handful chopped Italian parsley
salt & pepper to taste

Sauce:
3/4 cup light mayonnaise
1/4 cup sour cream
3 tablespoons red wine vinegar

▶ Cook tortellini in salted water until al dente. Drain. Rinse with cold water and drain again. Place in bowl.

▶ Add next five ingredients and gently stir together.

▶ Whisk sauce ingredients together and add to tortellini. Mix well. Chill.

▶ Serves 6-8

Travel Tip Refrigerate salad overnight, or at least two hours before packing in cooler.

Harkness Memorial State Park
Waterford

After counting thirty-three Things To Do in the "Harkness Brochure," it is no surprise that on a weekend afternoon in July we find that visitors have already filled the picnic tables. In addition, spaces under the shade trees have been staked out and the tiny beach area is draped with chairs and towels, even though swimming is not allowed.

Still, there is plenty of open space for an un-crowded feeling at this 234-acre park, and we quickly join in some of the suggested activities, such as: fish, fly kites, play with the dog, gaze out to sea, watch boats sail by, have a birthday party. Some folks even enjoy activities that are not on the list, like exploring, napping, and board games. Later, on our way back to the parking lot, we see two happy toddlers riding their tricycles on the wide walkways. The activities seem endless at this popular state park; in fact, if we had stuck around, we would have caught a glimpse of the wedding party that was due in a couple of hours. Yes, "Get married!" is on the list.

The Italianate mansion, built in 1906, is a perfect setting for such an event, with open, airy rooms and spacious windows that provide spectacular views of the terrace, gardens, and Long Island Sound in the distance. We are just in time to take the last guided tour of the mansion before the wedding preparations begin. The rooms are mostly bare of furnishings, and rather than being a disappointment, it is an opportunity to concentrate on the impressive architecture. Old photographs help bring the mansion to life, as does the information that the tour guide shares concerning the remarkable history of the Harkness Estate and the generous family who owned it.

Harkness Memorial State Park

Address: 275 Great Neck Road, Waterford, CT 06385.
Telephone: (860) 443-5725.
Website: www. ct.gov/dep/site. Click Outdoor Recreation; click State Parks & Forests; click Quick Links.
Hours: Daily 8 am–sunset. Mansion Tours: Sat, Sun & Holidays from Memorial Day W/E to Labor Day 10–2:15. Gift Shop: Fri–Sun 12–4.
Parking Fee: W/E & Holidays: CT res. $7; non-res. $10; after 4 pm $5. Weekdays: CT res. $5; non-res. $7; after 4 pm $5. (no fee for Mansion tour).
Directions: From Hartford area, Route 91 S to Route 9 S to Route 95 N, Exit 75. Bear right at end of exit onto Route 1. Proceed 3 miles to the light at Avery La. (Route 213), turn right and follow to park. Avery La. will become Great Neck Rd. Park is on right. (Check website for additional directions.)

Another Harkness activity not to be missed is "Enjoy the gardens," which were designed by Beatrix Farrand, a renowned pioneer in garden landscaping. The Italian garden, with its eye-catching design, fountain, and sculpture, is on the west end of the mansion. After some time is spent meandering along the stone walkway and admiring the rich hues of the flowering plants, we explore narrow pathways to find hidden delights, such as a tiny fish pond and an iron sculpture. The Oriental garden on the east side is recognizable by its wrought iron entrance and statuary, enhanced by a sunken garden with pool and fountain.

Upon leaving the mansion and the gardens, walk down the gravel path, keeping to the right. Take the middle path into a garden on your right—look for a large round stone flower urn. Just beyond the urn is an endearing pet cemetery. It is enveloped and hidden from view by five Japanese maples, their elongated, gnarled branches twisting and turning upward, stripped of foliage except for the tips forming a near perfect, lacy green umbrella. What a peaceful, private hideaway for the five small headstones etched with names and dates of deceased family pets.

When exiting the garden, continue walking away from the mansion to the Carriage House, where on weekends, you will find a small, charming gift shop run by the Friends of Harkness, an organization that is dedicated to the restoration and preservation of the Estate. The Friends' current project is the restoration of the greenhouse.

▶ The Picnic

Harkness, in my opinion, is one of the best destinations in Connecticut for a full-scale day trip, with its wide range of versatile activities and its spaciousness. Harkness also lends itself to a grand picnic. After all, "Picnic" does hold the number one position in the brochure under suggested activities.

In this hurried world we live in, even our leisure time is taken in small doses. This is the perfect time and the perfect place to treat yourself and your favorite people to an entire day of one-part relaxation and one-part fun. We have an elaborate picnic planned for the occasion.

Although there are numerous picnic tables about the grounds, you will need to arrive early on a weekend or holiday in order to grab one of the upright charcoal grills scattered about. Choose a table in the shade to keep the food safe. There will be plenty of opportunities to soak in the sun as you are touring around.

In the event you don't get an early start or would prefer to have a cold picnic, simply spread your cloth anywhere on the expansive lawn, either under a shade tree or in the open sunshine. Or, bring your folding chair down to the beach and enjoy a picnic with a view of Long Island Sound.

Personal preference is the key here; no matter which activities or picnic options we choose during our visit, we always have a memorable day at Harkness.

▸ What's In Our Picnic Basket?

▸ **Antipasto Platter**

Grilled Pork Tenderloin

Favorite Sides

▸ **Cheesy Garlic Bread**

Cupcakes

Fresh Cherries

Cheesy Garlic Bread

This bread goes well with almost any meat cooked on the grill. The warm savory cheese and spices bring pleasure with every bite.

1/4 cup butter

1/4 cup sweet onion, minced

2 garlic cloves, minced

1/4 teaspoon dried oregano

1/8 teaspoon ground cumin

1/8 teaspoon (or less) red pepper

3/4 cup reduced fat Mexican 4
    cheese, shredded

1 loaf Italian bread

▸ Melt butter in small pan over med-high heat. Add onion; sauté 2 minutes. Add garlic and stir for 30 seconds. Stir in spices.

▸ Split Italian bread lengthwise and brush butter mixture on both halves. Sprinkle cheese evenly over butter and press together.

▸ Double wrap in aluminum foil and place on grill, away from direct heat, until warm and cheese is melted, turning once. (Depending on heat of grill, it will take about 15-20 minutes.) Slice bread into desired thickness.

Travel Tip This bread can be prepared the night before and stored in the refrigerator, then transferred to cooler. It will take longer to heat if going straight from the refrigerator or cooler to the grill.

▶ **Antipasto Platter**

Antipasto Platter

I had such fun assembling the ultimate antipasto platter for a recent family picnic. The discount stores had a good selection of colorful plastic dishware, and I selected a 24X16 inch platter, white with wide slanted edges in a bright raspberry. Two plastic ice cream dishes in lime green placed in opposite corners made a pretty picture. Here is what the antipasto platter consisted of:

Green, orange, and yellow whole peppers were carefully shaved on the bottom, as needed to stand straight, then hollowed out and placed in the opposite corners and middle of the tray, making a diagonal row. I put **carrot sticks** in the green pepper, **burgundy olives** in the yellow pepper, and **stuffed green olives** in the orange pepper. (Next time, I may put a dip in one of the peppers, with the other two holding carrot and celery sticks.) Each of the peppers were placed on one large **Boston lettuce leaf**. In the opposite corners were the two ice cream dishes, one holding bright **cherry tomatoes**, and the other, **marinated mushroom caps**. Somewhere in the middle, a pile of **sweet roasted peppers** sat atop a group of **lettuce leaves**. The color palate was complete.

Now, it was time to think about heartier fare, and the rolling, stabbing, stacking, and threading began, followed by the placement of each item on top of more lettuce leaves set amongst the bowls and peppers. First, one-pound of **ham** and one-pound of **Swiss cheese** were rolled up together, slice by slice, the ham on the outside and the cheese on the inside. I cut each one in half—or if you use the long ham slices, cut in thirds. A pound of **hard salami** was simply folded over, piece by piece, piled in two stacks and fanned out. A stick of **pepperoni** was sliced into one-quarter to one-half inch slices and threaded on colored plastic picks, with a small cube of **Cheddar cheese**, then another pepperoni slice. When I got tired of threading, I simply scattered the rest of the pepperoni slices and cheese squares around to fill up empty spaces. I bought some **cheese twists** (mozzarella and soft cheddar) and partially separated the top of each twist into three or four pieces, pulling each piece down about 2 inches to form a curly top. I placed these in two piles.

Finally, I added sprigs of **fresh parsley** here and there and a clear container of colorful plastic toothpicks. The bright and enticing platter attracted a lot of attention!

The platter can be as big or as small as your party dictates. Don't be afraid to add and delete ingredients to include your own favorite finger foods. The one described here was set on a buffet table at a party for about 20 and there were leftovers.

Recommendation for maximum enjoyment—if this platter is served as an appetizer, set it out well before your main course. If you are barbecuing, let guests munch on the antipasto while the grill heats up and the meal is cooking. If you put the platter out with everything else, hungry folk will simply head for the more hearty fare and ignore your beautiful platter. Also, make sure it is not placed in the sun, otherwise everything will go limp pretty fast.

Travel Tip My picnic was on a house patio, but if I was traveling any distance, I would simply have cut, rolled, and threaded the items at home, put everything in separate containers and carried to the picnic site in a cooler. It doesn't take long to assemble the tray once everything is planned and prepared ahead of time. From then on, it's just plain fun!

Mark Twain House & Museum
Hartford

At age 35, Samuel Clemens, a.k.a. Mark Twain, a.k.a. "a man of words" visited Hartford, Connecticut to discuss *The Innocents Abroad* with his publisher. In a letter to Olivia Langdon, his fiancée, he wrote, "Puritans are mighty straight-laced and they won't let me smoke in the parlor, but the Almighty don't make any better people." Hartford was well-known as one of America's most prosperous cities, but something else touched Twain. "You do not know what beauty is if you have not been here."

So, it is not surprising that soon after, Mark Twain and Olivia, would decide to build a home in Hartford, in a literary portion of the city called Nook Farm. Here, he would write some of his greatest works: *The Adventures of Tom Sawyer,* loosely based on his own childhood, *Adventures of Huckleberry Finn,* written as a Treatise on racism rather than the sequel to *The Adventures of Tom Sawyer* that was originally planned, and *A Connecticut Yankee in King Arthur's Court.*

The house was quite radical for the period and The Hartford Daily Times wrote "…it is one of the oddest looking buildings in the State ever designed for a dwelling, if not in the whole country." After describing the rooms on each floor, the article ended with "The novelty displayed in the architecture of the building, the oddity of its internal arrangement, and the fame of its owner, will all conspire to make it a house of note for a long time to come." Yes, indeed!

During our tour, the rooms, and in fact the entire house, vividly come to life as one listens to spirited stories about the occupants. Mark Twain's presence is especially felt in the 3rd floor study or billiards room. This is the room where Twain

Mark Twain House & Museum

Address: 351 Farmington Ave., Hartford, CT 06105
Telephone: (860) 247-0998
Website: www.marktwainhouse.org.
Hours: Mon–Sat 9:30–5:30; Sun 12–5:30. Jan–Mar closed Tue. Closed major holidays.
Admission: Adults $13; Seniors (over 65) $11; Children (6-16) $8 Under 6 free. Note: A new Kitchen and Servants Wing Tour $3 if purchased with a tour of the house.
Directions: From I-84, Exit 46 (Sisson Ave. in Hartford) At light, turn right onto Sisson. Continue four blocks to end. Turn right onto Farmington Ave. Continue three blocks and look for sign on right at entrance to Museum's free parking lot. (Note: Entrance to parking lot is one block before the Mark Twain House.)

ultimately did most of his writing, deliberately placing his desk in a corner position so he wouldn't be tempted to sit and stare at the lovely scene just outside the window. When he wasn't working this was also the place, we are told, "to drink, smoke, swear and hang out with his friends." Listening to the endearing stories about Twain, with his larger-than-life personality, lovely Olivia, refined and well-bred, and darling daughters, Susy, Clara, and Jean, we begin to understand what Twain meant when he said of the house, "It had a heart and soul…"

After your tour of the house, we recommend visiting the Museum Center to view art and objects reflecting Twain's life. The Paige typesetting machine that Twain invested in so heavily and which was at least partly responsible for his bankruptcy is especially interesting. We also watch a short biography in the theater. Here, my favorite story was when Twain started wearing a white suit year-round in public. He was 71, and called it his "dontcareadamnsuit," which made sure he lived up to his reputation of being colorful, playful, and extremely opinionated. We would add beloved.

The well-stocked museum shop, one of the best in the state, is not to be missed. We found tons of books about and by Mark Twain, but there is so much more — truly unique gifts for every taste and budget.

▶ The Picnic

As we walk from the parking lot to the flight of stairs leading into the museum, we notice a nice expanse of grass on our left that would make for a pleasant lawn picnic, reminiscent of those that were enjoyed by Mark Twain and his family during the 1880s. In the present time, however, the next best thing about this spot is that it is close to our car. After the tour there are only a few steps to walk to retrieve the picnic basket.

In the summer, you may also opt to picnic on the patio adjacent to the second floor café. Although the patio is only accessible through the café —and someone must be willing to go back to the car for the picnic — once there, you will find a pleasant retreat with plenty of tables and chairs conducive to a relaxing lunch.

Of course, if you visit during December, when the house is embellished in gifts and garlands for a Victorian Christmas, you will no doubt enjoy a "picnic" of eclectic sandwiches and salads in the Café.

Wherever you decide to picnic, you will be happy that you stepped back in time at the home of one of America's best-known authors.

▶ What's In Our Picnic Basket?

▶ Cold Lobster Salad Roll
Coleslaw
Salt and Vinegar Chips

Max Fish is the newest addition to the Max Restaurant Group. Other restaurants include Max Amoré, Max Downtown, Trumbull Kitchen, Max a Mia, Max's Oyster Bar, Max's Tavern, and Max's Catering. Visit www.maxrestaurantgroup.com.

Cold Lobster Salad Roll

(Courtesy of Adam Alderin, Chef at Max Fish)

4 1 pound lobsters or 1 pound picked lobster meat
6 oz Mayo
3 stems celery
3 each shallots
1/2 bunch parsley
Dash of Tabasco
Dash of paprika
Salt and pepper
4 split top buns

Notes: If using store bought lobster begin at step three.

Steps:

1. If using whole lobster cook in boiling water for eight minutes, and then cool under running water.

2. Once chilled pick lobster meat out of shell and rinse under water to clean.

3. Small dice celery and shallots.

4. Chop parsley till fine in size.

5. In mixing bowl add all the ingredients but lobster and blend together with spoon.

6. Carefully fold in chilled lobster meat and mix well, taste and adjust seasoning with salt and pepper.

7. Pack in airtight container and keep chilled.

8. Assemble on site, in a split top hot dog bun place lobster salad, best served with salt and vinegar chips and coleslaw.

▸ Serves 4

Roseland Cottage
Woodstock

From the minute I park the car and step outside, I know it is going to be a memorable day. The sun is shining and the resident mocking bird greets and serenades me all the way to the Carriage House. Inside, friendly staff members are welcoming, and the Bowen's "company drink," pink lemonade, has been prepared for thirsty visitors. During the tour, the guide shares a wealth of information about the pink house, the garden, and the fascinating Henry Bowen himself.

Imagine it is July 4, 1870. You are in the town of Woodstock, Connecticut, one of thousands of invited guests at the home of the man known throughout the country as "Mr. Fourth of July." The guest of honor at this year's event is President Grant, who will make a speech advocating abolition. Later, the festivities include lawn games, socializing, and an assortment of refreshments. Almond macaroons and pitchers of pink lemonade are certain to be included.

Of course, you are at the summer home of Henry C. Bowen, where every Fourth of July gathering featured a guest of honor. He entertained four Presidents here, as well as other politicians, all Republican, of course. In fact, there is a proclamation by his attorney and friend, President Lincoln, honoring Bowen for the work he did as one of the founders of the Republican Party.

Henry Bowen amassed his fortune soon after leaving the Woodstock home where he was raised. After settling in New York City, he worked in textiles for four years before striking out on his own as a silk merchant. Soon after, he courted and won the affection of his former boss's daughter, Lucy Tappen. They had ten children together and Henry continued his entrepreneurial ventures, founding an insurance company and publishing newspapers.

Roseland Cottage

Address: Route 169, Woodstock, CT 06281.
Telephone: (860) 928-4074.
Website: www. historic newengland.org. Click Historic Properties and Places to Visit. Also check out Programs and Events.
Hours: June 1–Oct 15 Wed–Sun 11–4. Tours on the hour.
Cost: Adults $8; Seniors $7; Children (6-12) $4.
Directions: I-395 to Exit 97, turn onto Route 44 west for 1 mile, west on Route 171; when it merges with Route 169 north continue on Route 169 for 1.5 miles. House is on left.

Nineteenth-century architect Joseph C. Wells, originator of the Gothic Revival style, built the striking pink home in 1846, fashioned after the cathedrals of Europe. The Bowens chose their favorite flower, the rose, as inspiration for the color of their home. The pink house color represents the petals and the brown window trim and green shutters suggest the branches and the leaves. Forever-after known as "the pink house," it has never been painted any other color, although the shade has changed thirteen times through the years, ranging from lavender to bubble gum. Finally, a paint analysis was able to determine that the present shade of coral-salmon most closely resembles the shade the Bowens used in 1888.

We discover that Roseland Cottage is all about authenticity. Inside the home, most of the elegant wall coverings and furnishings are either original or from subsequent family owners. The dining room table is set with the Bowen's personally-inscribed rose-colored Limoges china, as if they are about to host a dinner party. The Preservation of New England Antiquities, owners of Roseland Cottage, recently renovated an upstairs bedroom where we see personal items belonging to Lucy, including her donated wedding dress.

Every bit as grand as the pink cottage, the Victorian parterre garden is an exact replica of the Bowens' 1850 garden, thanks to the discovery of a plant list from that year. Dwarf boxwood borders the twenty-one flowerbeds, all separated by pathways, but the real attention-grabber is a large oval bed that emulates the design of an oriental rug. It is even more striking when looking at it from an upstairs window. This is thought to be the only boxwood parterre garden in New England.

Later, Pam Russo, the helpful site manager, locates a recipe for the Almond Macaroons that were most likely enjoyed at the Fourth of July parties. So, what are we waiting for—let's picnic!

Visitors are encouraged to stroll around the spacious grounds either before or after the tour to investigate additional buildings and to enjoy not only the flowers, but also the magnificent trees. And, of course, to picnic.

On this perfect June day, we choose a bench in front of the garden with a view of the pink cottage. In the event of inclement weather, an alternative is a table in the Carriage Barn, providing there are no functions going on.

Although I did not have the authentic Bowen recipe for almond macaroons prior to my visit, you may want to include these cookies in your Roseland Cottage picnic. Add pink lemonade, to toast the Bowens, just as dignitaries and friends must have done at the Fourth of July parties those many years ago.

Ham & Cheese Sandwiches

▶ **Three Bean Salad**

▶ **Almond Macaroons**

Pink Lemonade (See Index for Lemonade Recipe)

Three Bean Salad

(Courtesy of Terry Bernard)

When I asked my friend to create a new three bean salad for me, she came up with this recipe. It's great.

1/2 pound green beans, ends trimmed and cut in half

1/2 pound wax beans, ends trimmed and cut in half

1 cup cooked garbanzo beans (if using canned beans rinse and drain)

1/2 cup sliced celery

1 cup grape or cherry tomatoes, halved or quartered

1/4 cup red onion, chopped

Dressing:

1/2 cup extra virgin olive oil

4 tablespoons balsamic vinegar

1 tablespoon light brown sugar

1/2 teaspoon salt

dash of pepper

▶ In a large pot of boiling water, cook green and wax beans about 5 minutes or until crisp-tender. Drain, rinse in cold water and drain again. When beans are completely cool, put all vegetables in a large bowl.

▶ In separate container, whisk or shake together all dressing ingredients.

▶ Just before serving, add enough dressing to the vegetables for personal taste. Toss.

▶ Yield: 6 servings

▶ Almond Macaroons

Almond Macaroons

(Courtesy of Pam Russo, Site Manager, Roseland Cottage)

This recipe is copied from Miss Leslie's New Cook Book, dated 1873, which Ellen Bowen used during a portion of her lifetime. The inscription in the book reads, "Mrs. H.C.Bowen, October 15, 1894." Note: Ellen Bowen was William Bowen's second wife.

The day before they are wanted, prepare three quarters of a pound of shelled sweet almonds, and a quarter of a pound of shelled bitter almonds; by scalding, blanching, and pounding them to a smooth paste in a marble mortar, (one or two at a time) adding, as you proceed, rose-water to prevent their oiling, and becoming dark and heavy. Having beaten to a stiff froth the whites of six eggs, and prepared a pound of powdered loaf sugar, beat the sugar into the egg a spoonful at a time. Then mix in gradually the pounded almonds, and add a grated nutmeg. Stir the whole very hard, and form the mixture into small round balls. Then flatten slightly the surface of each. Butter slightly some shallow tin pans. Place the macaroons not so close as to be in danger of touching; and glaze them lightly with a little beaten white of egg. Put them into a brisk oven, and bake them a light brown.

The following recipe is my own interpretation and modernization of the 1873 recipe. I was not prepared for how tasty these cookies are—crunchy on the outside and sweet and chewy on the inside.

Almond Macaroons

1/2 pound almonds
3 egg whites
1 cup granulated sugar
1/2 teaspoon nutmeg

▸ Preheat over to 375 degrees F.

▸ In an electric blender or food processor, grind almonds to a fine powder. Set aside.

▸ Beat egg whites with electric mixer until stiff peaks form.
Add sugar very gradually while continuing to beat on medium speed.
Fold in ground almonds and nutmeg.

▸ Batter will be soft. Spread in a 13x9-inch pan that has been greased and floured.
Bake for approximately 15 minutes or until set. They will be very light brown.
Cool pan on rack. When cookies are cool, cut into 1-1/2-inch squares.

▸ Yield: 4-1/2 dozen

MYSTIC SNAPSHOT

Mystic is Connecticut's best-known tourist attraction, enticing visitors from every corner of the state and, in fact, from all over the world.

They come to Mystic Seaport and Mystic Aquarium, the nation's leading maritime and marine life museums, and to Olde Mistick Village, a colonial New England village with more than sixty stores and restaurants. They come to historic Main Street to browse in the shops, pausing to watch the tall ships pass under the ancient draw-bridge. They stroll along the paths of a peaceful and serene nature center, and kayak on the busy Mystic River.

Whatever the interest—cultural, artistic, or physical—it can be found in Mystic. And, because Mystic is all about growing, expanding, and improving what is already pretty spectacular, visitors will always be able to make their own discoveries, just as this author has been doing for more than thirty years.

What about the picnicking facilities? For the most part, they don't shout out "Here I am" but are prone to take second stage to the activities. Perhaps this is as it should be here in Mystic, when you consider the fine seafood restaurants available in the area. Yet, their subtle presence provides a good alternative to restaurants, particularly for families with small children, folks on a budget, or anyone with dietary restrictions. Or someone like me, who simply loves to picnic!

Mystic Seaport

Mystic Seaport, the nation's leading maritime museum, is a recreated nineteenth-century New England village of trade shops, homes, and tall ships. This seventeen-acre coastal location includes galleries, both indoor and outdoor exhibits, and demonstrations of everyday life during that period. Add a planetarium and a research library, and the list goes on.

One of the most popular exhibits at Mystic Seaport is the *Charles W. Morgan*, the last wooden whaleship of its kind. This National Historic Landmark was built in New Bedford, Massachusetts, in 1841. It is great fun to explore the ship and interact with the knowledgeable guides on board. Another tall ship worth visiting is the *L. A. Dunton*, an American fishing schooner launched in Gloucester, Massachusetts in 1921. And, at the Preservation Shipyard, there is a visitor's gallery and a collection of more than 500 historic wooden vessels, the largest in the country.

If by now you have a hankering to be captain of your own historic wooden boat, visit the Boathouse at Lighthouse Point. A rowboat or sailboat may be rented and launched on the Mystic River. Or, if you'd rather be a passenger, make arrangements for a half-hour cruise aboard the *Sabino*, a coal-fired steamboat built in 1908.

This museum works hard to offer its visitors an accurate view of the once lucrative shipbuilding industry in Mystic, and the daily life of the residents whose entire existence was influenced by the sea. Are they successful? Well, if it wasn't for the visitors walking around in tank tops, sunglasses, and baseball caps, we might believe we really had been magically transported back a couple of centuries. The authenticity of the buildings and maritime

Mystic Seaport

Address:
75 Greenmanville Avenue, Mystic, CT 06355.
Telephone:
(888) 973-2767.
Website:
www.mysticseaport.org.
Hours: Apr–Oct 9–5; Nov–Mar 10–4; closed Christmas Eve and Christmas Day.
Admission: Adults $18.50; Seniors (over 65), Active duty military and college students $16.50; Children (6–17) $13; Age 5 and under free.
* Ticket may be used for a second consecutive day when validated.
Directions: From Interstate 95 (north or south), Exit 90. Proceed south on Route 27, about one mile. Seaport will be on your right, parking on left. Look for signs.

exhibits are clearly evident, and even the appearance and speech of some of the museum employees belie the fact that they are actually living in the twenty-first century.

In addition to all the permanent attractions at Mystic Seaport, more than 160 major events and educational programs take place each year, so there is a good chance that whenever you plan your visit, something out of the ordinary will happen.

Today is July 4th and I have brought friends visiting from England to the Seaport. We are delightfully surprised by an old-fashioned parade with red, white, and blue decorated buggies and other nineteenth-century paraphernalia. Adults and children alike are dressed in costumes of the period, and visitors are encouraged to join the parade. I don't know about anyone else, but marching music always starts my feet tapping.

▶ **FYI:**
The Museum Store is not your typical museum shop. The two floors in the 6,000 square foot building contain the nation's most complete collection of maritime books, as well as reproductions from Seaport collections, and an impressive collection of photography. Even with all the classic items, plus clothing and a Country Store, there is still a good assortment of souvenirs for the kids. Note that there is "street" access to this store and entrance to the Seaport is not essential.

▶ The Picnic

We do not see any picnic tables at Mystic Seaport. Presumably, it is because there are several options for purchasing food. And, on this day, there are no lawn picnickers either, although there is plenty of open space.

Because there are just three of us, we opt to picnic on one of the many benches scattered about the Village Green. Our menu consists of simple finger foods that were easily transferred from the cooler to a small canvas bag before we entered the Seaport.

After rest and sustenance, we continue our tour of the Seaport. There is still so much to see!

► **Salami, Provolone &
Tuna Roll-ups**

Grapes

Salami, Provolone & Tuna Roll-ups

The compatible filling is rolled up and baked in refrigerated crescent rolls. Either straight from the oven or the refrigerator, these roll-up slices make a great appetizer, snack, or accompaniment to a soup or salad lunch.

1 package refrigerated
   crescent rolls
1 package (4.5-oz.) thin sliced Genoa
   salami (about 3-1/2-inch rounds)
1 package (8-oz.) Provolone slices
   (about 4-1/2-inch rounds)
1 can (6-oz.) white tuna in water

1 tablespoon mayonnaise
1 tablespoon sour cream
1/4 teaspoon Dijon mustard
1/4 teaspoon fresh lemon juice
salt and pepper to taste

► Prepare tuna: In small bowl, flake tuna with fork.

► Mix together: mayonnaise, sour cream, mustard, lemon juice and spices. Add to tuna. Set bowl aside.

- Preheat over to 350 degrees F.

- Unroll dough and separate into four pieces. Working with two pieces at a time, place side by side on a flour-covered surface. Pinch perforated edges together to seal. Use your fingers to spread the dough to a 7x7-inch square.

- Place 1-1/2 slices of provolone across center of dough. Place 6 slices of salami over the provolone, overlapping slightly. Spread one-half of the tuna mixture across the bottom two-thirds of the salami. Starting at the bottom, roll up. Place seam side down on lightly greased baking sheet. Pinch the sides of the dough together.

- Bake for 12 minutes or until dough is golden brown.

- Yield: 2 rolls, each roll providing fourteen 1/2-inch slices.

Travel Tip Carry to the picnic site straight from the oven by wrapping in aluminum foil or towels and placing in an insulated container. The rolls will keep warm for 2–3 hours. You can also let the rolls cool and place in the refrigerator overnight. Transfer to a cooler before leaving for your destination.

Mystic Aquarium & Institute for Exploration

Mystic Aquarium, a marine science center dedicated to education and research, features a diverse group of oceanic animals from around the world. Marine mammals, such as dolphins and sharks, are very much in evidence here, as are the only beluga whales in New England.

If you haven't visited Mystic Aquarium in recent years, expect to be impressed. The Immersion Theater offers a daily schedule of mysteries from the sea: An interactive dolphin program, the latest information discovered about the Titanic, or live broadcasts from an exploratory undersea laboratory. Check out the new Fluorescent Coral Exhibit, engaging not only in appearance but also in its scientific research data, and visit the Ray Touch Pool where you can reach in to touch cow nose rays..

Peer through the huge center pool to view all sizes of colorful and exotic fish. Smile back at the sociable beluga whales, or make prior reservations to enter a beluga pool for actual hands-on contact with these marine mammals, weighing anywhere from 1,000 to 1,750 pounds. Visit the live sea lion show in the Marine Theater, and then get eye to eye with the penguins in their pavilion.

The newest attraction, "Birds of the Outback," is a 1,200 square foot aviary housing hundreds of birds native to Australia. Visitors can feed the birds as they perch on arms and shoulders looking for a hand-out.

Each day, the Aquarium posts the various feeding times, so when visitors enter the gates they can plan their tour accordingly. The fun of observing the feeding process up close is one of the highlights of the Aquarium. Among the choices are beluga whales, penguins, fur seals, and sea lions.

Mystic Aquarium & Institute for Exploration

Address: 55 Coogan Boulevard, Mystic, CT 06355.
Telephone: (860) 572-5955.
Website: www.mysticaquarium.org.
Hours: Mar–Nov everday 9–6; Dec–Feb Mon–Fri 10–5, Sat, Sun & Holidays, 9–6; Closed Thanksgiving and Christmas Day. Note: last admission 1 hour before closing.
Admission: Mar–Oct: Adults $22; Seniors (65+) $20; Children (3-17) $17; Age 2 and under free. Nov–Feb: Adults $19.50; Seniors (65+) $18.50; Children (3-17) $14.50; Age 2 and under free. Note: Aviary extra $2 * Tickets may be used for three consecutive days when validated.
Directions: From Interstate 95 (north or south) to Exit 90. Proceed south on Route 27. Take first left onto Coogan Boulevard (Steak Loft Restaurant intersection). Pass Olde Mistick Village. Aquarium is on left.

Today, we are at the outdoor Seal Island at feeding time.
It is fascinating to watch the antics of the seals as they climb in and out of the water to accept their fishy lunch from the hands of a trainer. This particular complex covers 2.5 acres, and various pools contain five species of seals and sea lions. Although they are all at home here in Mystic, they could be anywhere along the New England Coast, the California Coast, or the Pribilof Islands of Alaska, so accurately has the Aquarium recreated their various native habitats.

The picnic facilities may not be fancy or scenic, but it's all about convenience at Mystic Aquarium. The small designated picnic area, with twelve metal tables and benches, is comfortable enough for visitors to enjoy a picnic before, after, or even in the middle of all the activities. It is located past the entrance, near the east end of the parking lot.

▶ What's In Our Picnic Basket?

Baked Chips

Tuna Salad Sandwich

Cut Up Veggies & Dip

▶ **Double Chocolate Banana Cake**

Double Chocolate Banana Cake

This fudgy cake is so rich it needs no topping other than sprinkled confectioners sugar, if desired. For ease, carry it to the picnic site in the baking pan and enjoy a delicious finale to your meal.

6 tablespoons (3/4 stick) butter

2 ounces unsweetened
   chocolate squares

2 or 3 ripe bananas
   (approximately 1 cup mashed)

1/2 cup vanilla yogurt

2 eggs, slightly whisked

1 teaspoon vanilla extract

1 cup flour

1 cup sugar

1/2 teaspoon baking soda

1/2 cup semi-sweet mini chocolate
   chip morsels

▸ Preheat oven to 350 degrees F. Grease and flour an 8-inch square baking pan.

▸ In a large saucepan over low heat, melt butter and chocolate squares, stirring constantly. Remove from heat. Add bananas, yogurt, eggs, and vanilla extract and mix thoroughly. In separate bowl, combine flour, sugar and baking soda. Add dry ingredients to wet ingredients; stir until blended. Fold in chocolate chip morsels.

▸ Pour batter into pan. Bake for 35-40 minutes, or until a tester or toothpick inserted in the center comes out clean. Cool in pan on rack for 15 minutes. Remove cake from pan and finish cooling on the rack. Replace in clean pan to transport.

▸ Serves 8-10

 **Travel Tip** This cake freezes well, and can be made ahead and lifted out of freezer before leaving for your picnic.

Olde Mistick Village

This 22-acre early American village is an unparalleled shopping experience, with inviting signs leading us down picturesque paths to more than sixty specialty shops. Each one thrives in its own free-standing wooden structure set among green lawns, flowering trees and gardens, and a duck pond. Several wooden platforms scattered throughout the village contain inviting benches for visitors to pause and enjoy the fragrant surroundings.

We move from one interesting shop to another, anxious to find the perfect gift for a mutual friend's birthday, and we are not disappointed. In addition to the anticipated assortment of fine clothing, accessories, gifts, jewelry, and kitchenware, there are shops for collectible dolls, kites, Christmas accessories, early American primitive furnishings, woodcarvings, nautical items, gourmet foods, and probably anything else we could want. Of course, since this is an early American village, there is also a General Store, always a favorite.

In addition to the everyday ambiance, special activities are scheduled throughout the year, such as Arts and Crafts shows, free summer concerts, and a spectacular light display during the Christmas holiday, all listed in a brochure that will be mailed upon request.

Olde Mistick Village

Address: Coogan Boulevard, Mystic, CT 06355.
Telephone: (860) 536-4941.
Website: www.oldemistickvillage.com.
Hours: Year-round: Mon–Sat 10–6; Sun 11–5, except Summer & holiday season: Mon–Sat 10–8; Sun 11–5. Closed major holidays.
Directions: From Interstate 95 (north or south) Exit 90. Proceed south on Route 27, first left onto Coogan Boulevard (Steak Loft Restaurant intersection), left at the crest of hill into Village.

After we stroll through the Village visiting the shops that interest us, we are ready for our picnic. Even on this busy Saturday, there are empty benches, and while I retrieve the cooler from the car, my friend guards our picnic space. Before long, we are enjoying a light lunch and getting re-energized for whatever comes next in our Mystic day.

▶ Ultimate Tuna Wrap
Seasonal Fresh Fruit

Ultimate Tuna Wrap

This recipe really perks up a can of tuna. Not only do all the extra ingredients give tuna a snappy new taste, it is also very satisfying.

6 Tortillas

2 cans (6-ounce) white tuna in water

1 can (8-ounce) crushed pineapple

1/2 cup light cheddar cheese, shredded

4 slices cooked bacon, diced or crumbled

1/4 cup diced celery

1/4 cup chopped onion

salt and pepper to taste

1/2 cup mayonnaise

2 tablespoons bottled low-fat honey Dijon salad dressing

2 tablespoons reserved pineapple juice

Boston (or your favorite) lettuce leaves

- ▶ Drain both cans tuna and put in bowl.
- ▶ Drain pineapple, reserving juice. Add to tuna.
- ▶ Add cheese, bacon, celery, onion, salt and pepper. Mix together.

- In separate bowl, whisk together the mayonnaise, salad dressing and pineapple juice.
- Add most or all to tuna bowl, mixing well. Chill.
- On each tortilla, place lettuce leaves, then spread about 4 rounded tablespoons of tuna mixture in middle of tortillas. Roll up.
- Yield: 5–6 tuna wraps

Option: 1/2 cup chopped walnuts or pecans may be substituted for the bacon.

Travel Tip Refrigerate salad overnight or at least two hours before preparing wraps. Place wraps in cooler for transport.

Downtown Mystic

Downtown Mystic is many things: historic, charming, distinctive, courtly yet welcoming, and of course, seafaring. But, the one thing Mystic is not, is a town. Mystic is a location, nestled between the towns of Stonington on the east side of the Mystic River and Groton on the west side. The hub of downtown is Main Street (Route 1) where it crosses the river.

There are three favorite activities in Downtown Mystic, so whether we have one hour or an entire afternoon to enjoy this location, we manage to fit them all in and are content before going on our way.

The Drawbridge – At forty minutes past the hour, we watch traffic and pedestrians come to a halt as a loud whistle announces the opening of the antique bascule drawbridge to let the tall ships pass through. It is fascinating to watch this massive steel structure do its job, squeaking and groaning from the effort. We are able to time it so we are at the Stonington end of the bridge (look for the very tall flagpole) rather than the Groton end where the busy stores are situated. Here, sitting on one of the benches along the pier, we have a good view of the ships cruising back and forth under the bridge.

The Stores – After enjoying the role of spectator for a while, we cross the bridge to join the shoppers and browsers strolling down one side of West Main Street and up the other. It is always a pleasant surprise to find a relatively small area with such a versatile array of shops.

Mystic Drawbridge Ice Cream Shoppe - Located right next to the drawbridge, we cannot pass by without stopping in for some of the tastiest ice cream around, made right on the

Downtown Mystic

Directions: From Interstate 95 (north or south) to Exit 90, south on Route 27, right onto East Main St (Route 1). **Parking:** Look for on-street parking on Route 1, on side streets leading up to bridge, or cross the bridge and look for parking lots. Store hours: varies from store to store and season to season. Generally open most days.

premises. It appears that few others can walk by either, especially in the summer when lines go right out the door. It is worth the wait, however, and gives us time to consider all the unique flavors listed on the giant wall menu. When we get our ice cream cones, the choice is either to grab a table inside or enjoy our licks while continuing to walk.

▶ The Picnic

Back at the Stonington end of the bridge, Mystic River Park is located adjacent to the river, just behind the benches where we watch the boats during the opening of the drawbridge. Although this is a relatively small park, there is plenty of grass on which to spread a blanket, especially since the majority of visitors seem to be in the vicinity of the shops on the other side of the bridge. Consult the Welcome Center for special performances in the park during the summer.

Crab Salad Finger Roll Sandwich
(**With Spinach Leaves**)

▶ **Cranberry Herbal Iced Tea**
(**Mystic Drawbridge Ice Cream**)

Cranberry Herbal Iced Tea

My sister Pat gave me this iced tea recipe several years ago. The best thing about it, besides its great taste, is the fun of trying different variations.

3 cups cranberry juice cocktail
6 orange & spice tea bags
1/4 cup sugar
1 quart soda water

▶ Bring juice to boil. Remove from heat, add tea bags and brew for 5 minutes. Remove tea bags. Stir in sugar until dissolved. Cool slightly, then refrigerate.

▶ Carry the iced tea and the soda water separately. When serving, combine one-half tea and one-half soda water. Serve with ice cubes.

▶ This recipe makes 6-7 eight-ounce glasses of tea when mixed with the soda water.

▶ For one glass: use 1/2 cup juice, 1 tea bag and 1 tablespoon sugar. Combine with 1/2 cup soda water.

Options: Substitute cran-raspberry or other variations of cranberry juice. Substitute orange almond tea or even a fruit tea.

Denison Pequotsepos Nature Center

After visiting some of the more lively and crowded attractions in Mystic, it is a welcome change to spend some time at this charming nature center.

Our exploration begins with a walk along some of the eight miles of trails in the 300-acre preserve. The melody of songbirds and gurgling streams along with the aroma of wild-flowers awaken our senses, as our meandering takes us across meadows, around a pond, over brooks, and through forestland. Later, we visit the hawks and owls living in roomy enclosures on the sanctuary property.

Entering the museum, we find that much of the outside environment has been re-created inside for our further enjoyment and education. Woodland, wetland, and meadow exhibits introduce visitors to the plant and animal life found in each habitat. Full size interactive displays, live animals, and the "Night in the Meadow" theater are especially appealing to the children. A rare, old exhibit of more than 200 mounted bird specimens is alluring for both experienced and budding birders.

The Nature Center Store overflows with choice items to complement the setting. Popular Field Guides and numerous nature books are in ample supply. Everything for the birds can be found, such as birdhouses, birdbaths, bird feeders, and birdseed, as well as a nice variety of nature-inspired smaller gift items.

This museum's roster of special programs and events is both ambitious and distinct. Along with the programs you might expect at a nature center, like naturalist-led walks on Saturday afternoons, there are creative activities for everyone. Bug Safaris and Scavenger Hunts are geared to children, while families are

Denison Pequotsepos Nature Center

Address:
109 Pequotsepos Road, Mystic, CT 06355.
Telephone:
(860) 536-1216.
Website: www.dpnc.org.
Hours: Mon–Sat 9–5; Sun 10–4.
Closed major holidays.
Admission: Adults $6; Seniors (65 +) $4; Children (12 & under) $4.
Directions: From Interstate 95 (north or south), Exit 90. Proceed on Route 27 North, travel less than 1/2 mile, turn right onto Jerry Browne Road. At 3-way stop turn right onto Pequotsepos Road, then travel 1/2 mile to sharp curve. DPNC is on left after curve.

offered Full Moon Hikes and overnight programs called "What Goes Bump in the Night."

Adults may enjoy a full moon paddle or the popular Wild Mushroom Festival, which originally began as a mushroom identification hike. Over the years, the activity grew to include participants bringing wild mushroom dishes to share, then to a workshop and picnic. The current fall festival still offers the mushroom identification hike, but in addition, there are specialty dishes prepared on-site by local chefs. Participants can enjoy samples while sipping wine, beer, or cider, listening to music, and gathering recipes. At the marketplace, folks have the opportunity to learn about wild mushrooms from the experts. As Maggie Jones, the executive director says, "Wild mushrooms have an aura of mystique and folks want to be educated as to the good, bad, and yummy."

One activity that we attended recently was held at the Peace Sanctuary on River Road. The early evening Lady's Slipper Walk, followed by wine and dessert, was the perfect interlude to cure the blahs and boost the spirit. Call for a calendar of events or check the website.

▶ **FYI:**
Check out the website's extensive list of questions and answers about wildlife, many having to do with personal contact or home invasion. Just click on "FAQ" at the top of the page.

During a prior visit, we chose to walk a few feet to the pond for a bench picnic. Not as comfortable as a table, perhaps, but when given a choice of eating locations, I almost always choose one with a view of the water.

Today, however, there is a busload of boisterous school children scavenging around the pond. We observe them for a while, intrigued by their enthusiastic search for slimy, slithering creatures. But the thought that they might actually catch one while we are eating prompts us to walk back to the museum.

Here, we have a choice of several tables arranged in the wooded areas around the building. It is perfect.

▶ **Wild Mushroom and Oyster Chowder**

Rolls

Fruit

During the course of my conversation with Maggie about the Mushroom Festival, she said she had a great soup recipe using wild mushrooms. I asked her to send it to me for my readers, and here it is!

Wild Mushroom and Oyster Chowder

(Courtesy of Maggie Jones, Executive Director, Denison Pequotsepos Nature Center)

1 lb Wild Mushrooms (I like a combination of hen of the Woods, oyster mushrooms + chanterelles)
3-4 cups chicken stock
1 QT of shucked oysters with their liquid
4 Tablespoons unsalted butter
2 Tablespoon Extra Virgin Olive Oil
2 leeks (white part), well cleaned and chopped
1 medium onion, diced
4 cloves of garlic, diced fine
2 bay leaves
1-1/2 teaspoons fresh thyme (1/2 tsp dried) or winter savory
3 Tablespoons of flour
2 cups milk or 1/2 + 1/2 (or, for a richer chowder, use cream)
Black pepper, freshly ground and red pepper flakes
Salt
Parsley, chives, and/or dill, chopped for garnish

- Heat oysters in their liquid with the chicken stock until barely cooked (the oysters will just start to curl). Remove oysters with a slotted spoon and reserve, then strain the stock through a fine strainer or cheesecloth, and set aside.

- Carefully remove any grit or soil from the wild mushrooms. Slice about 1/3 of the mushrooms by hand, and finely chop the remainder in a food processor.

- In a cast iron skillet, melt 1 Tablespoon of the butter in olive oil. Add the leek, garlic and onions and cook until onions are translucent (about 5 minutes), then add bay leaves, thyme (and/or savory) and both the sliced and finely chopped mushrooms. Reduce heat and cook for 10-15 minutes.

- In a large pot, melt the rest of the butter. Sprinkle in the flour while stirring with a wire whisk to make a roux. Cook for just a minute, then slowly pour in the hot stock, stirring continually. When the liquid is slightly thickened, add the mushroom mixture and simmer for 1/2 hour. (You can stop here and refrigerate the mixture for a couple of days before finishing, if you like to do things ahead).

- About 1/2 hour before serving add the milk or cream, and heat just to a simmer, dice the oysters and add to the soup. Season with salt and freshly ground black pepper and red pepper to taste. Remove bay leaves and serve with chopped fresh herbs.

- Servings—Main Course: 6-8

Note: Many types of wild mushrooms are available dried. For a more intense mushroom flavor, you may incorporate some dried mushrooms and the liquid used to reconstitute them. If you cannot find fresh wild mushrooms, you can use store bought mushrooms and add a few dried mushrooms for flavor, but be careful not to overpower the splendid oyster taste.

Mystic River Kayaking

To kayak on Mystic River for the first time is to discover a busy, thriving waterway peacefully co-existing with a tranquil natural landscape.

We rent the kayaks right around the corner from the drawbridge, and in mere minutes of donning our life jackets and shoving off, we are within shouting distance of the ships moored at Mystic Seaport.

When we turn around, it looks like we can paddle forever. Slipping first under the Mystic drawbridge, then the railroad bridge, we pass Mason's Island and almost reach Abbott's Lobster in the Rough in Noank before deciding to turn back.

All along the self-guided tour, we enjoy a close-up view of the various boats traveling alongside us as well as those moored at docks and boatyards. Amidst all the boating activity, the charming waterfront homes and various inlets also grab our attention, and by the end of the trip, there is no doubt there will be many more explorations on this charming river.

▶ **FYI:**
The first time we went kayaking, we received only verbal instructions about the best route to take. The next time, we were prepared with a large, colorful map picked up in the Welcome Center, also available in stores.

Mystic River Kayaking

Kayak Rental: Mystic River Kayak, 15 Holmes Street, Mystic, CT 06355. **Telephone:** (860) 536-8381. **Hours:** Memorial Day W/E to end of Sept Mon–Thurs 10–6; Fri–Sun 9–6. (Subject to Change. Call first). **Cost:** Single: 1 hr $20; 2 hrs $30; 4 hrs $40; 8 hrs $60. Double: 1 hr $30; 2 hrs $40; 4 hrs $50; 8 hrs $70. **Directions:** Follow directions to Downtown Mystic. Just before drawbridge turn right onto Holmes Street. Left driveway is just after S&P Oyster Co. restaurant on corner. (Park on street, walk up the driveway and to the right until you come to Mystic River Kayaking.)

T he suggested picnic site is the Mystic River Park described in the chapter "Downtown Mystic." Just across Main Street from the kayak rental, it is a convenient location to both relax and re-nourish after an exhilarating paddle.

> ## What's In Our Picnic Basket?

> ### Seafood Pasta Salad
> **(Served On A Bed Of Lettuce)**
> **European bread from grocers**

Seafood Pasta Salad

This salad was designed for its ease in preparation, so I didn't want to spoil the simplicity by spending a lot of time on elaborate dressing ingredients. The prepared dressing suits the salad perfectly; however, the balsamic was a bit "bitey" for my taste, so I softened it with a little tomato paste and sugar.

Recipe continued on next page.

SALAD:

1-1/2 cups uncooked penne pasta
1 cup feta cheese, crumbled
4 ounces cooked salad shrimp or
   medium shrimp cut in half
   (or 1 small can tiny shrimp rinsed
   and drained.)

1 small can (6-ounce) lump crabmeat,
   rinsed and drained
1/2 cup cherry tomatoes, halved
1/2 cup green bell pepper, diced
1/4 cup black olives, sliced (optional)
2 tablespoons scallions, sliced thin

▶ Cook pasta in salted boiling water until tender. Do not overcook. Rinse in cold water and drain. Place in bowl. Add rest of salad ingredients.

DRESSING:

1/2 cup bottled balsamic
vinaigrette dressing
1-2 teaspoons tomato paste to taste
1/2 teaspoon sugar

▶ Whisk together. Mix dressing into salad. Chill.

▶ This salad may be prepared the day before, but in this case, do not mix the dressing into the salad until packing your cooler.

▶ Serves 6-8

> ▶ **FYI:**
> Wondering what to do with the leftover tomato paste? Measure out tablespoons onto tin foil, which has been placed on a cookie sheet and put in freezer. When set, place in plastic storage bag and refreeze for future use.

More Mystic

Yes, there is an endless supply of activities waiting to be discovered by anyone with an enthusiastic and adventuresome spirit. I'll list just a few to get you started.

Williams Beach Park

Sometimes when we visit Mystic in the summer and take advantage of all the activities near the water, we actually want to get into the water. Just a short drive from the Mystic Bridge is Williams Beach Park, a sandy beach about 200 feet long. This small beach has some big enticements to draw people to its shore, like a convenient location, a small children's playground, and fantastic picnicking, including a covered pavilion with picnic tables, upright charcoal grills, and wonderful shade trees.

The Williams Beach Park is owned by the YMCA, and doesn't charge non-members to use the beach. However, there are no changing rooms or showers at the beach (there are restrooms) and there is a charge to use the facilities at the Y. Also, I am told that the summer months may be crowded with campers. But, check it out. You may hit it at just the right time.

Mystic Art Center

The Art Center, founded in 1913, has a lovely downtown location on the bank of the Mystic River. In addition to the galleries and studios, there are workshops, lectures, and classes for the whole family. If you are already browsing downtown, why not extend your walk to include regional art with your other activities. Just pass the shops on West Main Street and take a left on Water Street. The Art Center will be on the left.

More Mystic:

Williams Beach Park:
Open: Every day sunrise to sunset, no entrance fee.
Directions: Follow directions for Downtown Mystic, except turn left onto Route 1, then right onto Masons Island Road and another right just over bridge onto Harry Austin Drive. Pass the YMCA building and drive down the hill to the beach.

YMCA:
Hours: Mon–Thurs 5:30 am–10:00 pm; Fri 5:30 am–9:00 pm; Sat–Sun 7 am–6 pm.

Historic Homes

A few years ago I saw a walking map of historic homes and other points of interest, but when I inquired at the Welcome Center recently, I was told the map was out of print. Although there are many beautiful homes located along the drive to the Seaport on Route 27, I wanted to know about the homes within walking distance of downtown. A helpful and knowledgeable woman at the Chamber of Commerce said Gravel Street is the place to see the homes of whaling Captains. She added that seafaring men often brought back sketches of buildings seen during their travels. This clearly influenced the designs of the homes built here during that period. Gravel Street, just off West Main Street, runs along the Mystic River and, in fact, faces Mystic Seaport. Walking away from the bridge, take the first right after the stores.

Elm Grove Cemetery:

Thanks to the same woman at the Chamber, I made another discovery. The Elm Grove Cemetery is a Victorian cemetery that evidently has much to teach us about nature and history. The layout is unique, with the main road forming the trunk of a tree, and lanes veering off to form branches. Thanks to sailors who traveled to far away places, the grounds are filled with rare and diverse trees and plants brought back to Mystic. The marble and brick chapel with ornate leaded glass windows stands alongside the river and holds fifty people for weddings and other functions. Headstones with Egyptian, Greek, and Gothic architecture have interesting stories to tell just for the reading. This park-like setting, complete with fresh water pond and tidal pond, was enjoyed by Sunday strollers during the Victorian era. Today, Mystic visitors are encouraged to do the same.

Mystic Art Center:
Telephone:
(860) 536-7601.
Website:
www.mystic-art.org.
Hours: Daily 11–5 (except between shows). Call first if this is primary destination. Closed major holidays.
Directions & Parking: Follow directions for Downtown Mystic. If going straight to Art Center, cross over the Bascule Bridge, left onto Water St. Center will be on your left. Parking $2 (covers entrance fee).

Elm Grove Cemetery:
197 Greenmanville Avenue (Route 27). Open during daylight hours.
Directions: See directions for Seaport. The cemetery is before the Seaport, on the right, after Friendly's.

More

More cruises on the Mystic River, more art galleries, more unique shopping, more scenic walks, more of everything is here at Mystic! For information on any of these activities, as well as special events, like the dates for the well-known annual Mystic Outdoor Art Festival, visit or call the Visitor Information Center at Mistick Village or the Mystic Depot Welcome Center downtown.

> ▶ **Note:**
> Be cautious about scheduling too many Mystic attractions in one day. For instance, the Seaport and the Aquarium each need an entire day for maximum enjoyment. You may be able to combine a couple of the other activities, depending on your interest and stamina, but do remember to save time for serendipity.

Mystic Depot Welcome Center: At Mystic Depot. **Telephone:** (860) 572-1102. **Hours:** Everyday 10–4. **Directions:** Heading downtown on Route 27 south, take sharp right onto Roosevelt St (Angie's Pizza on corner). Take left into Train Depot.

Mystic & Shoreline Visitor Information Center: At Olde Mistick Village. **Telephone:** (860) 536-1641. **Website:** www.mystictravelsource.com. **Hours:** Everyday Mon–Sat 9:30–5 (summer months until 6 pm); Sun 10–5. Closed major holidays. **Directions:** Follow directions to Olde Mistick Village. From Coogan Boulevard, take first left into Village. Look for sign on right.

▶ The Picnic

Picnic almost anywhere the mood or the timing warrants. Even the platform at the Mystic Train Depot has a small table suitable for picnicking. And, the Mystic Depot Welcome Center is here, always the best place to begin your Mystic explorations.

Happy discoveries!

▶ What's In Our Picnic Basket?

Bacon, Lettuce & Tomato Sandwich

▶ Deviled Crab Stuffed Eggs

Star Mader Presents

themuffinmom@cox.net

Deviled Crab Stuffed Eggs

(Star Mader teaches cooking classes at West Hartford Adult Ed and at Wild Oats Market. Her philosophy about cooking is healthy, delicious and easy to make.)

(For 12 Deviled Eggs)

6 large to jumbo boiled eggs
1/2-2/3 cup crabmeat
    (or imitation crabmeat)
1-3 teaspoons sweet red pepper,
    finely diced
1-3 teaspoons chives or scallions,
    finely diced
1/4-1 teaspoon sea salt

dash black pepper
dash cayenne pepper
1/4 teaspoon tarragon
1/2-1 teaspoon parsley,
    finely chopped
1/2-1 teaspoon fresh lemon juice
1/4-1/2 cup mayonnaise

OPTIONAL

1/2-1 teaspoon Dijon mustard
paprika
chives

▶ Boil eggs and cool. Peel and cut in half. Poke out yoke into a medium size bowl and put whites on a serving platter.

▶ In food processor (with the puree blade on) or mixer, finely process 1/2 cup of the crabmeat. Add to egg yokes. Mash together until smooth. Add red pepper, chives, sea salt, black and cayenne pepper, tarragon, parsley, and lemon juice. Mix well. Add mustard and mayonnaise. Mix well.

▶ Put a 1/2-inch piece of the remaining 1/4 cup of crabmeat into the egg white and stuff with the egg yoke mixture. Use a teaspoon to stuff, or pipe mix into whites using a pastry bag.

▶ Top with paprika and chives.

Main Street
Essex

In our opinion, Essex has Connecticut's quintessential Main Street—lovely historic homes on an early 1800s tree-lined street, complete with white picket fences, American flags, and flower gardens lovingly cared for in small side lots or front yards.

This street also contains everything a resident could ever want or need. Okay, it doesn't have a movie theater or a gas station. But, it does have a post office, banks, bookstore, toy shop, clothing stores, gift and specialty stores, grocers, sandwich and ice cream shops, and restaurants, including the historic Griswold Inn. Oh yes, a church, a park, and even professionals and organizations, such as the Nature Conservancy have their offices here. All this and more co-exists amicably in hardly more than a one-half mile setting.

We park at the top of Main Street and stroll down one side and up the other, stopping in shops that intrigue us and just enjoying the quaintness of this picturesque village. There is a short diversion to our circuit, however, when we reach the foot of Main Street. The Essex Steamboat Dock, directly in front of us, causes us to pause for a view of the river, then when we make a quarter turn to the left we spot the Connecticut River Museum. Our curiosity leads us up the path to its door.

The museum has been a small treasure here for thirty years, but the warehouse building itself has quite a historic significance. It was built in 1878 for the steamboat traffic between Hartford and New York, replacing earlier commercial wharf structures dating back to 1650, when colonial ships traded with the West Indies. Imagine! The first American warship, the *Oliver Cromwell*, was built here during the Revolutionary War.

Main Street Essex

Directions: Interstates 95 or 91 to Route 9, exit 3. Follow signs to Essex Main Street.

Connecticut River Museum

Address: 67 Main Street, Essex, CT 06426.
Telephone: (860) 767-8269.
Website: www.ctrivermuseum.org.
Hours: Tue–Sun 10–5.
Admission: Adults $7; Seniors $6; Students $5; Children (6–12) $4; Age 5 & under free.

The exhibits, both changing and permanent, recount the history of the Connecticut River Valley and the influence that the river and the residents had on each other. Today, the first floor is taken up with an exhibit that examines the nineteenth century through the life of East Haddam's William Goodspeed.

Goodspeed, the owner of a steamboat line, had many interests. Among them was his love of theater, which in 1877 prompted him to build Goodspeed Opera House, the tallest, grandest, and most conspicuous structure along the river until well into the twentieth century. After his death in 1882, the "Victorian wedding cake," as the opera house was sometimes called, served a variety of odd uses, none of which were befitting this grand structure. Thankfully, in the late 1950s it was restored to the musical theater we enjoy today.

We like the way information is presented in a visitor-friendly manner through exhibits, a video, prints, and photographs. Come to think of it, everything about the Village of Essex is visitor friendly, just as it must have been 350 years ago.

Although our focus is on shopping (technically, the museum qualifies because it has a giftshop) there is so much more to Essex. No need to limit your meanderings to Main Street. Stroll down the village lanes to check out the marina and shipyard, or, for a more organized tour, pick up a Walking Map at the Connecticut River Museum. Just remember, the most strenuous activity here is "strolling." I guarantee you will not see a single soul hurrying or scurrying about—I think there is a town ordinance against it.

> ## ▶ FYI:
> Check out the RiverQuest, conveniently docked at the Connecticut River Museum. Numerous cruises along the lower Connecticut River include eagle cruises, bird cruises, and our favorite, a sunset picnic cruise. Check the museum website for more information. (Click River Tours.)

Essex Town Park snuggles right into the charm of industrial Main Street, situated on the west side of Main and leading down to Middle Cove, an estuary of the Connecticut River. There is a nice variety of trees in the park, all with name markers, and a pagoda complete with benches.

After our curiosities about this park are satisfied, we buy fresh peaches from the Farmers Market and are ready for lunch. Picnic tables are scattered about. We can picnic down by the water where it is relatively quiet except for the water lazily lapping against the moored sailboats, or in the middle of the park, just far enough from the sidewalk for a feeling of privacy yet close enough to be aware of the shoppers and street strollers. Hey, wait for us!

▶ What's In Our Picnic Basket?

Shrimp Cocktail
Gourmet Crackers
Garden Salad
▶ **Fresh Squeezed Lemonade**

Fresh Squeezed Lemonade

(Courtesy of Holly McCarthy)

Lemonade is the ultimate hot weather drink, and this recipe finds the perfect balance between sweet and tart. There is an added step with the syrup-making process, but the result is well worth the effort.

4-6 ripe lemons
1 cup water
1 cup sugar

▶ Wash lemons. Cut in half. Squeeze lemons to make 1 cup. Depending on the lemons, you may get less juice. If necessary, adjust the water and sugar accordingly. Set aside.

▶ Cut half of the squeezed lemons in slices and remove rinds.

▶ Put water and sugar in covered saucepan. Add rinds. Bring to a boil. Remove cover and simmer for 10 minutes.

▶ Remove from heat and cool. Strain into pitcher. Add the lemon juice and 5-1/2 cups cold water. Stir and refrigerate.

▶ Servings: 6 eight-ounce glasses.

See **Fun Alternatives** on next page.

✶ ✶ **Fun Alternative** ✶ ✶

For pink lemonade you can add a couple of drops of red food coloring. However, I prefer to add a teaspoon per glass of either maraschino cherry juice or cranberry juice cocktail. Either of these juices will alter the taste slightly, but it is a nice change on occasion.

✶ ✶ **Fun Alternative** ✶ ✶

While I was vacationing in England a few years ago, friends introduced me to a charming pub and a popular English drink. A Shandy is made with one-half light ale and one-half lemonade. Today, I like it even better, because unlike the English, I use fresh lemonade and lots and lots of ice. Now, if I could only duplicate the inviting pub atmosphere!

Marlborough Barn
Marlborough

This may be a "shopping picnic," but at Marlborough Barn it is also much more. As we wander through the Village, we discover treasures we didn't even know we wanted, oddities we have not seen anywhere else, and enough ideas to boggle the decorating mind.

The Old Country Store is a favorite, simply because there is something for everyone, from penny candy—now ten to twenty-five cents—to maple syrups and jams, pottery, placemats, unique utensils, fine china, and hand-fringed woven tablecloths in every size and color. Entire nooks and crannies are devoted to lamp-shades, baskets, silk and dried flowers, and colorful quilted bags in every size conceivable. Candles abound, not only in an area devoted to them, but also spilling over into rooms containing other specialties.

As we wend our way through the barn, the rooms seem to go on forever—the Dining Room Showcase, The White House, with bedroom and living room furniture, the Rug Gallery, and at the end, The Mill House, with additional home furnishings and accessories. Oh, and downstairs, somewhere in the middle (don't miss it) is The Holiday Shoppe. A separate building houses The Country House (furniture), the Curtain & Quilt Shop, and The Fireplace Shoppe.

New England Traditions Ltd is also in an unattached building and is a must see. At first glance it looks like an ordinary hardware store. But, as we examine the huge wall display of home accessories, such as towel bars and drawer pulls in all finishes and sizes, and paint in the unique colonial colors we cannot find in most paint stores, we feel like we have been taken back a century or two.

Marlborough Barn

Address: 45 North Main Street, Marlborough, CT 06447.
Telephone: (860) 295-8231 or (800)-852-8893.
Website: www.marlboroughbarn.com.
Hours: Tue–Sat 10–5; Fri 10–8; Sun 12–5. Closed major holidays.
Directions: From Route 2 traveling east , exit 12. Continue straight. Barn is 1.7 miles on right. From Route 2 traveling west, exit 13. Left off exit, first light turn right onto North Main St. Barn is just over hill on left.

Upstairs, we find a unique assortment of clocks, lamps and lighting fixtures, bird-baths, mailboxes, cupolas, and a variety of flags. My fascination here is with an entire table devoted to balancing toys, which I, like a child, cannot walk past without setting them all in motion. (Don't tell anyone!)

Each store in the complex is filled with beautiful, unique, and fine-quality items just waiting to be discovered. Antique and craft shows are among the Special Events scheduled on the grounds during the year. Dates can be confirmed on the website.

▶ The Picnic

Sadler's Ordinary Restaurant and Bakery is on the premises, and has been praised in many publications. So we won't talk about the fine food here. We'll simply say that although the majority of the picnics in this book are brought from home, who would deny that, on occasion, a purchased picnic might be enjoyed every bit as much. The restaurant has made it easy by placing three picnic tables outside and taking orders "to go."

Today, we brought our own food and used one of the two picnic tables next to the pond, although there is also lawn space on which to spread a picnic cloth. After lunch, the ambience of this country setting causes us to linger—but not for long. There is more shopping to do!

Cold Sliced Leftover Chicken
  or Roast Beef

▶ **Cold Marinated Asparagus**

Applesauce

Date Nut or Raisin Bread

Cold Marinated Asparagus

I designed this recipe especially for picnicking; it's delicious cold and can be made the night before. Although the prepared grated cheese works fine, whenever possible I grate fresh cheese for this dish.

1 pound asparagus
1 tablespoon olive oil
1 tablespoon balsamic vinegar
1 tablespoon water
1/2 teaspoon Dijon-style mustard

1/4 teaspoon sugar
1/8 teaspoon dry Italian seasoning
salt and pepper to taste
2 tablespoons Romano cheese, grated

▶ Wash asparagus, snap ends off and remove scales. Cook in a covered bowl in the microwave for 3-5 minutes or until fork tender. (Other cooking options are a steamer or saucepan on the stovetop.) Quickly drain and thoroughly rinse in cold water to stop the cooking process. Blot dry with paper towels and put in covered container. Set aside.

▶ Whisk next seven ingredients together—everything but the cheese—and pour over asparagus. Turn asparagus until covered with marinade. Refrigerate for at least two hours or overnight.

▶ Just before serving, sprinkle with the cheese.

▶ Makes 4-6 servings.

Connecticut Trolley Museum
East Windsor

F ounded in 1940, The Connecticut Trolley Museum is the nation's oldest incorporated organization dedicated to the preservation of streetcars. Its goal is to provide educational and historical information about the trolley era in New England from 1890 to 1945.

We wait for the trolley at the historic Isle of Safety, which was once located next to the Old State House in Hartford. The ride is one and one-half miles long, and at the end of the line the conductor gives us a brief history of our particular car. Then we turn around, well, that is, turn the seats around, to head back to the station.

Our first ride takes place in car No. 4. The conductor tells us the setting is Montreal in the 1920s. I imagine the women and girls dressed in their most fancy attire, wearing wide brim hats, necessary to shield the sun due to the open top. Today, even in jeans we feel elegant in this observation car, being only one of four built in the world. It still has the fancy iron scroll work on the front and sides and polished wooden seats that graduate upwards by varying floor levels, giving all 28 passengers an excellent view of the beautiful city sights.

Our next ride is in car No. 840, used to shuttle fans to the Yale Bowl in the 1940s. Known as an open air car, the open sides were perfect for packing in extra fans who would balance on the running board while holding onto polished poles.

Although we favor the open air cars more on this warm summer day—one conductor called it "natural air conditioning"—the closed cars are entertaining because of the vintage ad signs stretching from front to back on both sides, like "BT Babbitt's 1771 soap powder" and "2 in 1 shoe polish 10¢."

Connecticut Trolley Museum

Address: 58 North Road, East Windsor, CT 06088.
Telephone: (860) 627-6540.
Website: www.ct-trolley.org.
Open: Apr–mid June Sat & Sun; Mid June–Labor Day Wed–Mon; Sept Sat & Sun; Oct Fri-Sun; Nov closed. Dec–Winterfest and Jan–Mar, call or visit website for schedule.
Hours: Mon–Fri 10–5; Sat 10–5; Sun 12–5. Closed Tue.
Cost: Adults $8; Seniors (62 +) $7; Youth (2-12) $5; Under 2 free.
Directions: From Interstate 91, Exit 45, 3/4 mile east on Route 140.

Whatever trolley we find ourselves riding is exciting and informative, due in large part to the dedication of the volunteers who operate just about every phase of the Trolley Museum, from taking tickets and conducting to repairing the trolleys and sweeping the floors. Their love of trolleys is evident, whether they are sharing historical information about the museum or offering personal tidbits about a particular trolley car.

After we have our fill of rides, which are unlimited with the entrance fee, we meander into Kelly Barn to look at the "sleeping trolleys," then to the Fire Museum to see the antique fire apparatus. The oldest appears to be a fire sleigh dating back to 1894.

At the Visitor's Center and Trolley Terminal there are a couple of additional streetcars and a locomotive to investigate, plus a gift shop that piques our curiosity. Then, while the kids check out tables set up with puzzles and games, we walk around to look at historical photographs on the walls.

Be sure to check the website for possible discount vouchers and special events.

▶ The Picnic

Everything here is in close proximity. The Trolley Stop Restaurant, a boxcar eatery, offers an assortment of sandwiches and salads. Diners can eat inside or outdoors at picnic tables.

Today, however, we have all the picnic fixings except cold beverages, so we simply retrieve our basket from the car, purchase drinks at the snack bar, and choose our table. While we eat, we enjoy watching both people and trolleys coming and going, something we intend to do more often at this interesting museum.

▶ What's In Our Picnic Basket?

Barbecue Chicken

Favorite Salad

▶ **Best Ever Banana Nut Bread**

Fresh Cherries

Best Ever Banana Nut Bread

My Aunt Madeline's recipe dates back more than 75 years. If you like your bread sweet and moist, you will probably agree this really is the best.

3/4 cup butter	3/4 teaspoon baking soda
1-1/2 cups sugar	1/2 teaspoon salt
2 eggs	1 cup mashed bananas
1/4 cup sour cream	2 teaspoons vanilla
1-1/2 cups all-purpose flour	1 cup chopped walnuts

- ▶ Preheat oven to 350 degrees F.

- ▶ Cream butter and sugar. Add eggs and sour cream, mixing well. In another bowl, combine flour, baking soda and salt. Add this mix to creamed mixture alternately with the bananas. Stir in vanilla and nuts.

- ▶ Pour into greased and floured 9x5-inch loaf pan.

- ▶ Bake for 1 hour or until a toothpick inserted in the center comes out clean and bread breaks away slightly from the edge of pan. Cool in pan on wire rack for 15 minutes; remove from pan and finish cooling on rack.

Dinosaur State Park
Rocky Hill

Recipe for an adventure: Start with thirty pounds of plaster of Paris, three-quarters cup vegetable oil, rags, and a five-gallon bucket. Add three enthusiastic youngsters, ages 6 to 9, who are eagerly looking forward to making a cast of a 200-million-year-old footprint of Eubrontes. Toss in the "Excursion Planner"—the one who tries to whip up a simple recipe that calls for three *quarts* water and *ten* pounds plaster of Paris for each cast, but who instead fills the bucket with three *gallons* water, into which is poured *five* pounds plaster of Paris. The only way the Planner gets through this disaster is that she has done one smart thing. She has brought along one of the mommies, who quickly sizes up the Planner's inadequate reading of a simple recipe for casting dinosaur prints and takes over. Relieved of her measuring duties, the Planner is only too glad to retreat to the nearest hardware store for more plaster of Paris.

The casting area is a bit chaotic on this Tuesday afternoon in mid-August, with all six casts in use and people negotiating to be next in line. So, we have plenty of time to perfect our "recipe." Finally, it is our turn to stir, kneel, pour, and pat, and then simply wait for the creation to dry. The entire process takes between thirty and forty-five minutes, so multiplied by three it turns out to be the longest activity at the center. It is so worth it, however, as we watch each excited artist wait for his or her turn, help with the process, write initials and date on the casting, and wonder in anticipation what the finished product will look like. They are all perfect, and we gratefully thank the busy but patient park attendants who help out in this area.

The Exhibit Center by no means takes a back seat to the casting area. The 122-foot geodesic dome is home to one of the

---

Dinosaur State Park

Address: 400 West Street, Rocky Hill 06067.
Telephone: (860) 529-8423.
Website: www.ct.gov/dep/site. Click Outdoor Recreation; click State Parks and Forests; click Find a Park; (or use Quick Links).
Hours: Grounds: daily 9–4:30 except Thanksgiving, Christmas and New Year's Day. (Trails close at 4 pm). Exhibit Center: Tue–Sun 9–4:30. Track Casting: May 1–Oct 31 daily 9–3:30.
Exhibit Center Admission: Adults $5; Youth (6-12) $2; Children (5 & under) free.
Directions: Interstate 91 traveling South, Exit 23, left at exit ramp (right if traveling North.) Park is 1 mile on right.

largest dinosaur track sites in North America. Five hundred Eubrontes tracks, excavated in 1966, are displayed in a realistic setting created with special lighting and sound effects. (The first 1,500 were reburied for preservation and possible future display in a new building.) Although no bones were discovered, a full-scale model of Dilophosaurus, a close relative to Eubrontes, was erected in 1981, and a few years later Eubrontes was declared by the Legislature to be the official Connecticut State Fossil.

The additional exhibits and interactive displays manage to be both educational and fun, thereby assuring every member of the family an enjoyable experience. The store's expected assortment of dinosaur models, videos, books, tee shirts, and games are supplemented by bins of small odds and ends, which delight the younger children.

Outside, more than two miles of nature trails wind through wetlands, meadowland, and forestland, and after lunch we choose our trek along the red trail. The re-energized children skip along to look for the markers. The adults trail behind, soaking up nature's tranquility. At the end of both the trail and the day, promises are made to return soon to walk the blue and yellow trails and to spend more time at the wildflower and butterfly gardens.

> ▶ **Note:**
> The following materials are
> needed for each track casting:
> 1/4 cup cooking oil
> Cloth rags & paper towels
> Five-gallon plastic bucket
> Ten pounds of plaster-of-Paris
>   (no substitutions)

The picnic area, like the rest of the park, is well maintained and attractively situated. There are plenty of tables and upright charcoal grills in a mostly shady section of the park.

The challenge is keeping the children content long enough to prepare the table and lift the food out of the picnic basket. Trail Mix Cones filled with tasty and healthy snacks is the perfect solution.

The rest of the picnic is simple too, which turns out to be helpful, since the main focus is on eating quickly and hitting the nature trail. We may just discover some new dinosaur prints. Hey, you never know!

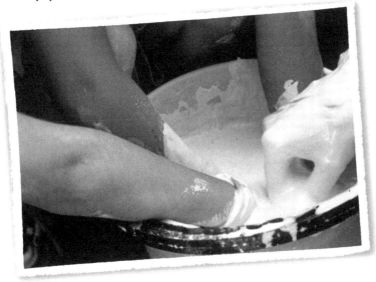

▶ Trail Mix Cones

Peanut Butter and Jelly Sandwich

Seasonal Fresh Fruit

Trail Mix Cones

These kid-friendly Trail Mix Cones come in handy while waiting for sandwiches to be made, or for any time a snack is needed.

Buy flat bottom ice cream cones and fill with favorite munchies. Some suggestions are:

Popcorn	Cereal
Raisins	Mini cheese crackers
Nuts	Dried fruit
Pretzels	Mini M&M's

▶ To transport, cover with plastic wrap and secure with a ribbon, string or elastic band. Pack standing upright.

▶ **FYI:**
Youngsters love to help assemble these cones. Just set the cones in muffin pans to keep upright while they alternately spoon in their favorite munchies.

Institute for American Indian Studies
Washington

The first thing we are invited to do when we walk into the IAIS building is view one of the short films about the early Algonkian Indians. This one focuses on hunting tools handcrafted with natural materials. It is interesting to see close-up views of an arrowhead, painstakingly formed and bound to the arrow, then finally adorned with feathers for the finishing touch.

One only has to tour the museum's exhibits to know that the Institute is successful in accomplishing its mission to serve "as a regional resource center for 10,000 years of rich American Indian culture as it applies to modern life through research, preservation, education and leadership."

Rare Indian artifacts are outstanding for their authenticity and educational value. Many of the Institute's artifacts are thousands of years old and were found nearby and in other areas of Connecticut. In addition, interpretive panels cover 12,000 years of prehistory and history in North America from the archaeologists' point of view.

One of our favorite displays is a re-creation of a longhouse. This dwelling would have accommodated two families, as evidenced by simple stone fireplaces at each end. One entire wall in the longhouse is a striking mural of the natives involved in everyday activities. Along with the arrowheads, animal skins, dried corn, pottery, and other artifacts, visitors get a glimpse into the life of Native Americans in New England.

In addition to the permanent exhibits, we enjoy the fine craftsmanship of the interim exhibits. On a prior occasion, there

Institute for American Indian Studies

Address: 38 Curtis Road, Washington, CT 06793.
Telephone: (860) 868-0518.
Website: www.birdstone.org.
Hours: Mon–Sat 10–5; Sun 12–5. Closed holidays.
Cost: Adults $5; Seniors $4.50; Children (up to16) $3.
Directions: Interstate I-84 Exit 15, Route 67 North to Route 199, left onto Curtis Road.

were accessories, including beaded bags, belts, moccasins, and intricately woven baskets. Today's display highlights deerskin dresses sewn together using a deer bone needle and thread made from the tendons of deer legs.

The Gift Shop is a continuation of the handcrafted items we admire in the museum, including baskets, books, jewelry, pottery, musical instruments, and weaponry.

Outside, a sign says, "Trail to Village." Along the trail we see a simulated archaeological site and at the end, the replicated seventeenth-century Algonkian Village. After examining the wigwams and the garden, we sit on one of the logs encircling a fireplace of stones, noting a sense of stillness, even with people coming and going. Although it was thousands of years ago that the Connecticut Indians had a practical and spiritual relationship with this land, the harmony is still felt today.

▶ **FYI:**
The website lists special programs, like the Family Archaeology Digs or the Village Interpreter Living History Program, when Native Americans come to the Algonkian Village Site to demonstrate traditional skills and answer questions about their culture.

I am happy to find that IAIS has placed a few picnic tables on the lawn in front of the Museum. During a prior visit, we sat on narrow wooden benches used for children's outdoor educational programs, although we did have the option of a tailgate picnic.

With the addition of tables, there is the opportunity to plan a more expansive and relaxing picnic. There is no desire to rush away from this tranquil environment.

Fishy Crackers
- **Grilled Kielbasa Sandwich**
- **Fresh Fruit Kabobs**

Grilled Kielbasa Sandwich

Grilled kielbasa has always been a favorite, and now that I created a zesty new sauce, I like it even better. A nice addition to this sandwich is sautéed onions and peppers.

1 kielbasa ring (approximately 1 pound)
Oblong rolls

SAUCE:
1 cup apple cider
2 tablespoons pure maple syrup
2 tablespoons catsup
1 tablespoon brown sugar
1 tablespoon orange juice concentrate
1 tablespoon corn starch

▶ Cut Kielbasa into four pieces. Cut each piece in half lengthwise creating 8 links.

▶ Whisk sauce ingredients together in a small saucepan. Bring to boil. Reduce heat and simmer for about 5 minutes, stirring occasionally. Cool slightly.

- Spread just enough sauce to cover bottom of a 13x9-inch pan or baking dish. Lay each piece of kielbasa on top of the sauce, skin side up. Brush additional sauce on top of kielbasa, reserving rest for sandwiches. Cover. Refrigerate for at least 2 hours or overnight.

- Grill or oven-broil kielbasa on each side. While kielbasa is cooking, heat extra sauce and spread on both sides of roll (may grill rolls first if eating at home). Place kielbasa in rolls with onions and peppers, if desired, and enjoy!

- Yield: 4–8 sandwiches (depending on thickness of roll and desired links).

Option: This recipe can also be used as an appetizer. Simply slice kielbasa into one-quarter inch slices and marinate in prepared sauce for 2 hours or overnight. Place on serving tray with a container of toothpicks.

Travel Tip Grill kielbasa and prepare sandwiches just before leaving for picnic site, wrapping well and carrying in insulated bag (carry sauce and onions and peppers separately and add just before eating). Or, grill kielbasa ahead and refrigerate. Carry everything in cooler separately and make cold sandwiches when ready.

Fresh Fruit Kabobs

These kabobs can easily be prepared the morning of your picnic and carried in a cooler to simply whisk out at whim. Enjoy as an appetizer while the rest of the meal is being prepared, as an accompaniment to the meal, or as a light dessert after the meal. They are also good as a snack between meals on a full day's outing. Fresh cut-up fruit must surely win the prize for the healthiest, most versatile picnic food.

Almost any sturdy fruit can be skewered. Some favorites are:

Apples	Grapes
Pears	Strawberries
Bananas	Pineapple (I sometimes use
Melon	canned chunks–my only
	exception to fresh fruit)

▶ Prepare the fruit by washing, peeling, hulling, etc. and cutting into similar size pieces.

▶ If peeling apples, pears or bananas beforehand, they must be coated with lemon juice to prevent browning—or pineapple juice (another benefit of canned pineapple.)

▶ Use 6-inch bamboo skewers. Arrange 4 or 5 pieces of fruit in a pleasing, colorful pattern on each skewer. Make sure the firmest fruits are on the ends to keep all the pieces secure.

✶ ✕ Fun Alternatives! ✕ ✶

Instead of fruit kabobs, place cut-up fruit in a bowl and set out with a container each of vanilla and strawberry-flavored yogurt. Add small bowls with a choice of toppings, such as granola cereal, chopped walnuts, banana chips, yogurt raisins, shredded coconut, raisins and honey graham cracker sticks.

Old New-Gate Prison & Copper Mine
East Granby

From 1707 to 1745, it was America's first chartered copper mine. In 1773, it became Connecticut's first state prison, named after the notorious prison of old London. Convicted criminals were confined here, including robbers, burglars, horse thieves, counterfeiters, and even Tories, those who supported the British cause in the American Revolution. The prison closed in 1827 when the prisoners were transferred to the new state prison in Wethersfield.

The modern stairway leading underground does not prepare us for what would today be considered barbaric living conditions. Cramped, damp, and dusky, it is difficult to imagine having to spend longer than a few minutes in this cavern. But the prisoners only climbed out once each day, up a rope ladder through a small opening and into the guardhouse. From there, they were escorted to workstations to produce nails, shoes, and barrels to pay for their keep. At the end of the day, they climbed back down into the cavern.

This self-guided tour leads us first to the lodging area, although the wooden "cabins" where the prisoners slept are no longer in evidence. The well containing the water supply is approximately forty-five feet underground, and the solitary confinement area, where prisoners were chained for improper behavior, is along a narrow tunnel.

The children love going in. I love coming out. The sunlight and fresh air are a welcome change as we walk around the grounds to view the prison buildings, mostly in ruins. But, we are able to enter one building to see exhibits depicting the history of Old New-Gate Prison, and a video filled with fascinating stories about

Old New-Gate Prison & Copper Mine

Address: 115 Newgate Road, East Granby, CT 06026.
Telephone: (860) 653-3563.
Website: www.eastgranby.com. Click on Old Newgate Prison on left.
Hours: Mid May–Oct Wed–Sun 10–4:30.
Admission: Adult $5; Seniors (60+) $4; College Student with ID $4; Children (6–17) $3; under 6 Free.
Directions: I-91N, exit 40, Route 20W through East Granby center to light on Newgate Road. Turn right on Newgate, go 1 mile.

the more colorful prisoners and their various attempts to escape. Our tour ends in the small gift shop, where we are unable to resist buying replicas of the first copper coin manufactured right here and the wrought iron key to the prison.

This national historic landmark is fascinating and informative, and will appeal to people of all ages, although babies and very small children may not appreciate going underground. The brochure advises that the temperature of the subterranean cells is a constant 52 degrees. I am glad I have a light sweater and comfortable walking shoes for the uneven and sometimes slightly slippery terrain.

Everything is in close proximity, so, not counting our picnic, a couple of hours is sufficient to see everything. That is, unless by happenstance, the visit is on a day when the Enfield Minute Men are re-enacting the life and times of the Revolutionary War. Then, it is twice the fun and twice the education.

The activity today is a muster, including a small fife and drum corps comprised of young children in traditional costume and a military unit taking part in a battle re-enactment. Eighteenth century muskets are carried by men dressed in reproduction clothing, authentic in color, style, and fabric, right down to counting the number of threads per square inch! Women at a nearby camp are cooking and sewing, while waiting for their husbands and sweethearts to return from battle. Other living history events held at New-Gate might include demonstrations by tradesmen, such as a blacksmith, basket maker, and cordwainer (shoemaker).

Viets Tavern, an unrestored mid-eighteenth century home originally owned by the first warden of New-Gate Prison, is located across the road. Prison guards often frequented the tavern during their free time. They would eat, drink, and play skittles, a game first introduced in England in the fourteenth century. Occasionally, the tavern is open to visitors for a self-guided tour or to test their skills at this historic game.

▶ **FYI:**
Although there is a hiking trail on the property, it has not been maintained and the staff does not recommend its use.

Hungry by now, it is time to escape to the other side of the massive, red sandstone wall that enclosed the prison compound to a green-lawned picnic area. A picnic table under a towering maple would provide summertime shade, but on this September day the preference is a table sitting in the late afternoon sun.

We enjoy our picnic with a view of the serene countryside.

▶ Turkey Panini Sandwiches
Raw Carrot and Celery Sticks

Cups of Prepared Jell-O or Pudding

Basket of Assorted Cookies

Turkey Panini Sandwiches

After enjoying this sandwich craze at restaurants for a couple of years, I finally got around to making my own Panini sandwiches at home. I prefer to buy a rotisserie cooked turkey breast or whole chicken and slice the breasts for this sandwich. Along with the Foccachia bread and the grilling, the fresh meat is what sets this sandwich apart from a deli sandwich.

1-8-inch round Foccachia bread

▶ Slice in half, then quarters; then slice each quarter in half lengthwise.

▶ Spread Cran-mayo dressing * on each slice, top and bottom.

Layer the following ingredients onto each of the four bottom halves:

spinach leaves
roasted turkey or
   chicken breast, sliced
Swiss cheese
roasted red peppers

▶ Add top of bread and grill in Sandwich Maker or fry pan.

▶ Makes 4 sandwiches.

* CRAN-MAYO DRESSING

▶ Whisk together to blend:

3 tablespoons mayonnaise

2 tablespoons jellied cranberry sauce

3 tablespoons finely chopped walnuts

1/4-teaspoon horseradish

dash of salt and pepper

Travel Tip If warm sandwiches are desired, grill right before leaving for your destination. Wrap well in aluminum foil and newspapers and carry in an insulated bag. Turkey Paninis also taste good cold. If the sandwiches are going to travel in the cooler, grill without the peppers and dressing. Carry these items separately and add just before eating.

Stamford Museum & Nature Center
Stamford

Even during the short walk from the parking area to Heckscher Farm, we imagine we could be in Puddle-by-on-the-Marsh, the town where Doctor Dolittle's practice became so successful after his parrot, Polynesia, taught him animal language. It is fascinating to watch the interaction between visitors and the animals and, yes, the animals do talk back.

It is very clear what the ducks are saying when they waddle out of the lake and up the bank to the picnic tables. They pick out a child holding a sandwich and quack loudly, while looking from the hand holding the sandwich to the child's face. As we tour the Hecksher Farm, we notice that the bunnies have a softer way of speaking to the youngsters, who scoop them up and trail their parents around the grounds, begging, "Can we take him home, pleeeze?"

When we check out the rest of the farm, we find barnyard birds, cattle and horse pastures, a pigsty, and fields for llama, sheep, goats, and bachelors (miniature donkeys, alpaca, rams, and bucks). Barnyard signs along the way amuse, entertain, and educate us about the residents.

During the summer months, this model working farm offers "Down on the Farm" programs that include animal grooming and feeding, gardening, and other related activities. On selected days during the week, a Farmer's Market sells farm fresh produce grown naturally.

Younger children love Nature's Playground, a unique outdoor space created from natural materials. While all the exuberant climbing, crawling, swinging, and sliding are going on, parents

Stamford Museum & Nature Center

Address: 39 Scofieldtown Road, Stamford, CT 06903.
Telephone: (203) 322-1646.
Website: www.stamfordmuseum.org.
Hours: Bendel Mansion & Galleries: Mon–Sat 9–5; Sun 11–5. Heckscher Farm: Daily 9–5 except Nov–Mar 9–4. Nature's Playground: Daily 9–5 (weather permitting) Closed major holidays.
Cost: Adults $8; Seniors $6; Students over age 17 $6; Children (4–17) $4.
Directions: Located 3/4 mile north of Merritt Parkway at junction of High Ridge Road (Route 137) and Scofieldtown Road. From Merritt Parkway, Exit 35, left onto High Ridge. From I-95, Exit 7 to Washington Boulevard, left onto High Ridge.

relax on the nearby porch swings. Distant voices waft in from some of the paths that trail through a mature forest of native plant species, also a habitat for a variety of mammals, birds, and assorted wildlife.

After we have our fill of nature, we walk up to the Main Building. The former Henri Bendel house was built in 1931 and modeled after two English Tudor style houses built in England. On the front lawn are four statues called the Four Seasons. A flyer challenges us to identify each of the "four seasons" without looking at the plaques, and after we study them for a moment, we are able to do so.

This building houses exhibition galleries, studios, classrooms, and a 50-seat planetarium, but we came to visit the Gallery of Changing Exhibits. The various collections are, in my opinion, unequal in their appeal and interest to all ages. The present exhibit, "Playing Around: Toys Designed by Artists," is comprised of fifty whimsical and imaginative pieces, all handmade and crafted from a variety of materials. Many are functional, according to the plaques, but alas, they are all displayed in glass cases, so we do not get to play.

As we enjoy the many aspects of this museum and nature center, it is obvious that everyone here, from workers and volunteers to visitors and animals, take great pleasure in these surroundings.

▶ **FYI:**
You can call ahead or go on-line for information on current exhibitions, as well as for the hours and cost of the state-of-the-art observatory, planetarium show, classes, and special events taking place throughout the year.

T he picnic area is in a pleasant and relaxing setting, with tables strategically placed under shade trees beside Laurel Lake. When we try to claim a table, however, we are told in no uncertain terms that rent, in the form of food, is expected.

So, we do the only thing we can under the circumstances. We wait until the attention of the demanding ducks is on the peanut butter and jelly sandwiches of young neighboring picnickers, then furtively unpack our own lunch and eat quickly, while keeping one eye on our new feathered friends.

Actually, the above is what I wrote during my first visit a few years ago. Today is relatively calm, perhaps because of the sign posted on a tree saying "Do not feed the ducks." At this moment anyway, boundaries seem to be distinct—ducks are swimming in the lake and visitors are picnicking at tables, and all are content.

▶ What's In Our Picnic Basket?

Rotisserie Chicken from Market

▶ My New Potato Salad

Tossed Salad

Pound Cake with

Fresh Strawberries

My New Potato Salad

A friend offered me a new potato salad recipe after I complained about being tired of the one I had been using for years. After making only slight variations to suit my taste, this potato salad recipe became my new favorite.

2 pounds red potatoes, boiled
  (with skins on)
1 medium sweet onion, chopped
3/4 cup mayonnaise
3/4 cup sour cream

1-2 teaspoons horseradish
3/4 teaspoon celery seed
1/2 teaspoon salt
1/2 cup fresh parsley, chopped

▶ Slice cooked, cooled potatoes into thin slices and put in large serving bowl. Mix remaining ingredients, except parsley, in smaller bowl. Pour most of dressing over potatoes and fold in completely. Add rest of dressing, or not, to suit taste. Top with parsley.

▶ Serves 6-8

 Travel Tip   Refrigerate salad overnight, or at least two hours before packing in cooler.

UConn Animal Barns
Storrs

Animal Barns - Greenhouses and Display Garden - Dairy Bar

The College of Agriculture was established at UConn in 1881. Today, with agriculture being the world's largest industry, animal science has expanded to include veterinary science, environmental health, nutrition, animal production, food science, biotechnology, and genetics.

Visitors are welcome to tour the Animal Barns and learn more about the animals that are cared for here, and families and children of all ages take advantage of this opportunity. During our many explorations at UConn, we learned that in addition to the Animal Barns there are other attractions that interest us, and now each visit has become a comfortable routine. There is nothing routine, however, about animals, plants, and yes, even (flavors of) ice cream, which makes each occasion unpredictable and entertaining.

We especially enjoy UConn in the spring, summer, and fall. Winter has an appeal as well, but the lower the temperature, the faster we move, which may mean eliminating the picnic and only visiting the animal barns and dairy bar. Hey, it's never too cold for ice cream!

Today, in early October, we are traveling east on Route 195 as we approach the campus. Just a short distance past the intersection of Route 44, we round a sharp curve and the campus appears in front of us. We begin our tour with the Animal Barns, which form a loop on Horsebarn Hill Road. The left turn comes up fast, and although the street is unmarked, it is just before the first barn.

University of Connecticut

Address: Storrs Road, Mansfield, CT 06268.
Telephone: Visitor's Center (860) 486-2000. Ice Cream Production Schedule: (860) 486-2634 or (860) 466-1021.
Website: www.canr.uconn.edu/ansci/barntours.htm.
Animal Barns: Open year-round, everyday 10–4.
Floriculture: Open year-round. Visitors: Mon–Thurs 9–4; Fri 9–3. Sales: Sept–Jun, Mon–Thurs 12:30–4; Fri 12:30–3.
Dairy Bar: Open everyday year-round except Thanksgiving, Christmas and New Years Day.
Hours: Dec–Feb 11–5 early closing on Christmas Eve and New Years Eve; Mar 11–6; Apr–May 11–7; Jun–Sep 11–8; Oct 11–7; Nov 11–6.
Directions: Heading east on Interstate 84, exit 68, right onto Route 195, 7 miles. Heading west on Interstate 84, exit 68, left onto Route 195, 7 miles.

The first barn houses poultry, but they are not allowed to have visitors so we continue on to the Kellogg Dairy Center. The ice cream we will eat later is made with milk from the cattle in this barn. Although it is too early to watch the one o'clock milking from the glassed-in area at the Visitor's Center, we stroll through the barn and wonder what the cattle are thinking when they stare at us with those big brown eyes.

Driving down the hill from the Dairy Center, we are mesmerized by the view of rolling green fields with white fences and trees as far as the eye can see. The foliage is about halfway to its peak autumn color and promises to be brilliant in a couple of weeks.

The next stop is the Cattle Resource Unit. Most of the cows are enjoying siesta— only three are still standing to feed. Outside, the calves are more fun. Unlike their staid elders, they are bouncing around, at least as much as they can within their confines. They remind us of toddlers on a "sugar high."

We drive on towards Livestock Unit II, the barn that houses the pigs used primarily for research. Although this barn is closed, we pull into the driveway to observe the sheep grazing next door. There are three varieties of ewes living at the University and, like all animals here, they help teach students the business of farming.

Next stop is the Livestock Unit I, a teaching and research facility that is home to the heifers, young cows that have not yet given birth. Then, almost at the end of the white fence is everyone's favorite animal—the horses.

We park on the side of a large red building and walk across the road and up the path to Horse Unit II, greeting the horses in various corrals. On the way back to the first corral, we see an amusing sight. Three horses are poking their heads out between the narrow slats in the fence, stretching their necks as far as they can to eat the grass. Yes, it really is greener on the other side!

The building next to the parking lot is the Horsebarn Hill Arena, and we stop to pick up a schedule of UConn polo. When it is discovered that the home games are on Sunday and are free, we promptly add this to our mental list of New Things to Do.

At this point, the decision must be made to either continue up the hill on foot or retrieve our car and drive up the hill to the Horse Unit 1. Today, we choose the latter. We always enjoy visiting the horse barn, but there is an added draw today. The outdoor Equestrian Center is bustling with horsewomen practicing their jumps, and we linger for a while to watch.

At the top of Horsebarn Hill Road, we turn right onto Route 195 to travel the short distance to "Floriculture," a brick building on the left. Both the driveway and the entrance to the six greenhouses are on the far side. One of the greenhouses has plants for sale, including beautiful, vibrant mums, reasonably priced considering the large size, and many smaller flowering plants. I finally choose a healthy-looking begonia with dark green leaves and peach blossoms, perfect for my office windowsill. We are told there is another greenhouse on North Eagleville Road specializing in exotic plants, but time is running out and we decide to save it for our next visit.

On the opposite side from the entrance to the building is a Display Garden with a wide variety of colorful flowers. I attempt to capture a photograph of one of the many Monarch butterflies, but they are too elusive as they flit from one blossom to another.

No visit to UConn is complete without the ultimate ice cream stop. The Dairy Bar has been a landmark on the Storrs campus for many years, and the sign across from the greenhouses never fails to entice us down the path. The menu boasts twenty-four flavors. Many are traditional, but today we choose from among the UConn flavors—Husky Tracks, Scholar Chip, and Jonathan Supreme, their specialty. Yum!

Although the ice cream is usually made in the early morning hours, we still like to walk back to peer through the observation window. The large stainless steel casks, sitting dark and silent, were whirling our favorite flavors just hours ago. If you are interested in watching the ice cream making process, there is a number you can call to find out the schedule. (Check the statistics on the "Activity" page.)

Back at the ice cream counter is a brochure entitled "Follow the Animal Trail," also found in some of the barns. Although written for children, the map of the barns and interesting animal facts appeal to adults as well. Note that the "Building List" begins with Horse Unit I, and if we were driving to UConn from the opposite direction (Mansfield), we would, no doubt, be accustomed to visiting the barns in the reverse order.

> ▶ **FYI:**
> Mileage from the beginning of the barn loop to the end of Horsebarn Hill Road is one and one-half miles. Back on Storrs Road (Route 195), mileage to the Floriculture and then to the Dairy Barn is about a half mile.

▶ The Picnic

There is no shortage of attractive surroundings and green grass for picnicking. A wonderfully enticing pond is a little farther along on Storrs Road (Route 195) from where we traveled today. Also, on our tour, we spot inviting benches—one nestled against pine trees beside Horse Unit I and another directly in front of the Display Garden.

If you prefer designated picnic areas with tables, there are two sites along the animal trail. At the bottom of the hill just before the bend in the road is a sunny and well-manicured space containing two picnic tables. A white fence that further extends along the entire bottom portion of the U-shaped animal barn loop sections it off. The second area is next to the horses at the other end of the fence. This one is larger, about 50 feet square, with two picnic tables and lots of shade trees.

Because this trip is one of our more spontaneous adventures, the contents of our picnic basket is determined by how well stocked the fridge happens to be. In addition, we often change the order of events, which then leads to a discussion about when to go for ice cream. My orderly and practical nature automatically dictates lunch first and then dessert, but the younger members of the group think otherwise. Occasionally, I do agree to reverse the routine, either because of convenience, or perhaps because of that long ago memory of "Backwards Day" at summer camp and the excitement of getting to eat dessert first!

Baked Chips

Pita Sandwiches, filled with leftovers from
   fridge or fixings from the deli

▸ **Hawaiian Coleslaw**

(UConn Dairy Bar Ice Cream)

Hawaiian Coleslaw

   I was experimenting with dressing ingredients for my coleslaw when I decided to add a can of crushed pineapple. The result—an exciting new recipe. Now, instead of coleslaw being merely a side dish habit, it's become a recipe of choice.

1-pound package of prepared coleslaw mix, chopped fine	2 tablespoons red wine vinegar
1/4 cup red onion, finely minced	1/2 cup mayonnaise
1 carrot shredded	2 tablespoons sugar
1 can (8-ounce) crushed pineapple, drained	1 teaspoon dry mustard
	3/4 teaspoon celery seed
	salt and pepper to taste

▸ In large bowl, combine coleslaw mix, onion and carrot.

▸ In small bowl, combine the next six ingredients, pineapple through celery seed. Blend and season with salt and pepper. Pour the dressing over the coleslaw and mix well. Chill.

▸ Serves 6-8

Note: This salad can be prepared a day or two ahead, and in fact, the blending of flavors improves the taste. Just keep cold by refrigeration and cooler until serving.

Spring
Wildflower
Hunt

Connecticut College Arboretum
(Native Plant Collection)
New London

At the entrance to the Arboretum's Native Plant Collection stands a tall iron fence in front of a curtain of foliage. Entering through the open black gates and standing at the beginning of the Laurel Walk is like stepping into a secret garden.

A perfectly groomed path, which slopes gently down a few hundred feet to the pond, is enclosed on both sides by Mountain Laurel in full white and pink bloom. Immediately, one feels protected, along with the 25-acre collection of trees, shrubs, and wildflowers native to eastern North America.

The Arboretum was established in 1931, beginning with the Native Plant Collection and the Caroline Black Garden. In the 1990s, the remaining college property, plus an earlier land acquisition, were designated as part of the Connecticut College Arboretum. Today, the Arboretum and the Physical Plant Grounds Staff maintain the 750 acres, providing Connecticut residents the opportunity to come here to study or simply admire the beauty of the landscape.

After picking up a map from the notice board at the entrance, we head down the path leading to "The Edgerton and Stengel Memorial Wildflower Garden." Because the deer have become a constant challenge as they rummage through the Arboretum seeking food, a wooden door leads into the garden. This year, especially, there are indications in other areas of the Arboretum that the deer are eating very well indeed.

Connecticut College Arboretum

Address: 270 Mohegan Avenue, New London, CT 06320.
Telephone: (860) 439-5020.
Website: http://arboretum.conncoll.edu.
Hours: Year-round from sunrise to sunset.
Location of the Native Plant Collection: The main entrance to Connecticut College is on the west side of Route 32, approximately one mile north of Interstate Route 95. Cross the campus to the Williams St. entrance and the Arboretum main gate. For more specific directions check website.
Parking: Park on Williams Street or in the South Parking Lot on the main campus.

Once inside, a boardwalk provides a sturdy path to view the wildflowers which are identified by markers. The markers are helpful for the wildflower hunt novice, but the more experienced enthusiast also enjoys the large variety. We like strolling in this woodland area, especially in late April or early May, the best time for the spring wild-flower collection. This year, however, it is the third Sunday in June before we arrive and our favorite wildflowers—great Solomon seal, yellow lady's slipper, jack-in-the-pulpit, purple and white trillium, and marsh marigold—are past bloom. The garden is lush and full, however, just as remembered, and the hunt is now on for late bloomers, such as iris and violets.

At some point during each visit to the Arboretum, the wildflower garden inevitably competes for attention with other areas. This year, it is the mountain laurel, first during the Laurel Walk, then later when we discover a grouping of larger, even more colorful plants. Never before have we seen such a fascinating variety in one area, hues ranging across a wide spectrum of deep reds, purples, oranges, and pinks.

In previous years we were lured away from the wildflowers to admire the pink and white flowering dogwoods, or to stroll between rows of giant birch trees with branches so long they almost brushed the earth. The birches, blighted by disease, have been gone for some time now, and I still miss them.

Yet, I know that "the only constant in life is change," and this is especially true in nature. At the Arboretum, an empty space is an opportunity for the staff to add new plants to the collection. For visitors, it is a time to take a different bend in the trail or to visit during a different season—late summer for the meadow's native grasses and wildflowers, October for the fall foliage and hydrangeas, and winter for the hollies and conifers. No matter when we visit, there is always something new waiting to be discovered.

▶ **FYI:**
You can call for brochures or go online to inquire about special programs, such as free guided tours in different areas of the Arboretum every Sunday from May through October, or for tours during specific seasons, such as Wildflower and Fall Foliage.

▶ **Note:**
Portable toilets can be found near Buck Lodge in the summer. Alternatives are an open Administration building on campus, or the Chapel, located on the street across from the Arboretum gate (the rear entrance to the College). The Chapel is lovely to see, in any event.

Although there are no areas specifically designated for picnicking, I have been encouraged on many occasions to enjoy a picnic anywhere on the grounds, and there are wonderful welcoming spots for this activity. Part of the charm of the Arboretum is that no one area is any more or less important than any other, and each individual space is simply part and parcel of an entire park devoted to the study and preservation of our natural surroundings.

Two sections within the Native Plant Collection have become favorites for picnicking. One is at the pond, which is a backdrop for the Outdoor Theatre. Provided that a Shakespearean or other theatrical event is not taking place, a picnic cloth can be spread anywhere on the expansive lawn, which doubles as seating for events.

Another favorite picnic place is inside a circular stone wall that was built as a memorial. The conifer collection surrounding part of the wall and the meadow beyond creates a calming stillness, and the wall itself provides a perfect seat for a casual picnic.

▶ Tabouli

Bagel or Pita Chips

Hard-Boiled Eggs, Quartered

Tabouli

(Courtesy of Mary Lou Wall)

I was skeptical when I first tried this dish at a friend's house, but I liked it so much, I went back for seconds. What a difference "home-made" makes. This recipe works equally well as a side, a main luncheon dish, or as an appetizer served with crackers or chips. For this picnic, try spooning Tabouli onto endive leaves.

> **1-1/2 cups bulgur wheat (found in Health Food Store or Organic section of supermarket)**
> **1-1/2 cups boiling water**

▶ Pour water over the bulgur wheat. Let sit in bowl while you chop vegetables.

Finely chop the following vegetables:

> **2 red peppers**
> **1 green pepper**
> **1 bunch scallions (whites only)**
> **3-4 tomatoes (scoop out seeds)**
> **3-4 stalks celery**
> **3/4 cup oil cured black olives, plain (found loose in Deli section of supermarket)**
> **4-5 large firm white mushroom caps (optional)**

Mix together in a large bowl:
3/4 cup olive oil
3-4 tablespoons garlic, minced
4-6 dashes Tabasco sauce (optional)
juice of 1 lemon

▸ Add the vegetables and bulgur wheat to bowl and mix everything together.

▸ Cover and put in refrigerator for 24-48 hours before serving.

▸ Servings: 6-10 (depending on whether it is served as a main dish or a side.)

Flanders Nature Center & Land Trust
Woodbury

A Spring Wildflower Hunt along the Botany Trail is ideal for folks who take their hunt seriously. During a visit in mid-May we identify thirty-five varieties, a number that far exceeds counts from similar areas. Perhaps, it is because a member of our group has packed three wildflower identification books in her backpack. I thought it was lunch!

This hunt also appeals to novices in the group. In fact, anyone who enjoys a spring walk will savor every step along the one-half mile woodland trail interspersed with a pond, streams, and open meadow. Wildflowers are everywhere, from the hearty phlox and violets adorning the edge of the trail to the lady slippers hiding in thickly-wooded areas and wild columbine flourishing near shaded rocks. Indeed, at every turn there is startling evidence of both the bounty and beauty of this nature center. My personal favorite is a cluster of painted trillium, the tip of each perfect white petal delicately brushed with a palette of pale pinks. What an exquisite contrast to the monochromatic woods and stone fence sharing this space.

Natalie Van Vleck, a farmer and artist whose mission was to preserve the natural environment, founded Flanders Nature Center in 1963. As the development of the Center was planned and the trails laid out, the area was landscaped with flora rescued from road building and suburban development.

The Pomperaug Valley Garden Club developed the Botany Trail in 1965, and members do an excellent job of maintaining the trail. Among other things, this involves the continuing rescue of wildflowers from land demolition and replanting at the Center for our enjoyment.

Flanders Nature Center (The VanVleck Santuary)

Address: 5 Church Hill Road, Woodbury, CT 06798.
Telephone: (203) 263-3711.
Website: www.flandersnaturecenter.org.
Hours: Office: Mon–Fri 9–5. Closed holidays. Trails: Daily from dawn to dusk year-round.
Directions to the Botany Trail: From Hartford, 84W to Exit 15, right onto Route 6 North for approx. 5 miles, left onto Flanders Road to Church Hill Road on right. The office is on the corner of Flanders Road and Church Hill Road. For the Botany Trail continue up Church Hill Road to the parking lot on the right. Look for the sign "Botany Trail."

There are six other trails on this property, all of which may be enjoyed seven days a week throughout the year. In addition, Flanders Nature Center continues to preserve the founder's mission by offering a wide variety of art and environmental programs for adults and children. Check out the seasonal activities, such as Maple Sugaring and the spectacular Fall Family Festival.

▶ **FYI:**

In Connecticut we can enjoy the bounty of Spring Wildflowers from the last week in April through the first week in June. The peak is generally the middle of May; however, even in our small state the climate is varied enough so that the peak may be as much as a week earlier or later.

After the Wildflower Hunt, we review our picnic options: grab the picnic basket and ground cloth from the car and walk back to the pond, have a tailgate picnic in the parking lot, or use the table in front of the Sugar House, just a few steps from the parking lot. (I inquired later, and yes, they do make maple syrup here, which is sold at the office.)

The picnic table turns out to be the best choice to recap our experience. While we are eating, the guidebooks are brought out to confirm and count the number of wildflowers identified on the trail. It is a sure thing that no matter how often we return to this or other trails, nature's canvas will have been rearranged, and the hunt will start anew. But, as of today, the Botany Trail goes on record as being our most successful wildflower hunt.

By the way, if you do not have your own wildflower expert to bring along, join one of the guided walks led by knowledgeable volunteers. Happy Hunting!

▶ What's In Our Picnic Basket?

▶ **Savory Baguette**
  ▶ **Sweet & Sour Meatballs**
     Fresh Apples or Pears, Quartered
     (Sprinkled with Lemon Juice
     to Prevent Browning)

Savory Baguette

A former neighbor introduced me to this quick and easy Baguette. She makes it for dinner when she gets home late from work and has it with a glass of wine. The next morning she eats the leftover for breakfast. I like it best warm from the oven, or even room temperature, as an accompaniment to a light dinner of meat and vegetables, or even cold leftovers—and the glass of wine.

1 organic multi-grain baguette	4 plum tomatoes
olive oil	salt and pepper
1 package (3-ounce) goat cheese	fresh basil, chopped

▶ Slice baguette in half and then slice both pieces in half lengthwise.
  This will produce four lengths of bread. Brush each bread length with olive oil.
  Crumble or spread one-quarter of the goat cheese on each length.
  Slice tomatoes in thin slices and place on top of goat cheese. Salt and pepper.

▶ Bake for 7-8 minutes or until warm in a pre-heated 350 degree F. oven.

▶ Remove from oven and sprinkle basil on top of tomatoes.

▶ Servings: Each bread length will serve between 1-2 persons depending on appetites and other foods served.

Travel Tip Wrap in tin foil and place in insulated bag for transport to picnic.

Farmington River Tubing
(Satan's River State Park)
New Hartford

W hat fun it is for an old-timer like me to go tubing down the Farmington River with five teenage grandchildren.

Located in Satan's Kingdom State Recreation Area, Farmington River Tubing has been in existence since 1979, and everything is organized in such a way as to make us feel comfortable and safe. From the pre-ride instructions to the lifeguards positioned at one of the rapids to the waiting shuttle bus to bring us back to our cars after the 2.5 mile, two-hour ride, I couldn't be more pleased.

As for the ride itself, three sets of rapids through white water provide just the right amount of thrills we crave. In between, there are periodic stretches of lazily drifting down the river while enjoying the serenity of the riverbanks, and an unexpected sighting of a small fawn positioned on the bank of the river as we float silently by. Serendipity!

Later, during our picnic, I ask my companions what they think I should tell readers about the experience. Here are their comments:

"Come on a sunny day." Although it is mid-July, the weather is cloudy and unseasonably cool. It is easier and infinitely more fun to cool off while on the river than to try to stay warm.

"Tell them to come after a rainfall." I hear a lot of "yeas" in agreement, knowing the kids are thinking the rapids would be more thrilling if the river was not so low from the recent drought. I agree, but for a different reason. I am still feeling the effect of a certain body part colliding with a sharp rock.

Farmington River Tubing

Address: Route 44, New Hartford, CT 06057.
Telephone: (860) 693-6465.
Website: www. farmingtonrivertubing. com. *Check website for age restrictions and additional information.
Hours: Memorial Day W/E to June everyday 10–5; July–Aug everyday 10–6; Labor Day W/E to mid Sept call for hours.
Cost: W/E & Holidays $20; Weekdays $18 (includes rental of tube and life jacket). Additional rides same day $10. Call for group discount rates.
Location: On Route 44, 7.5 miles from Intersection of Route 8, or 3 miles east of downtown New Hartford. Look for sign "Farmington River Tubing" and "Satan's Kingdom State Recreation Area." (Portable changing areas and portable restrooms are available.)

"Let them know that the calm water is great for playing." And it is! Were it not for my age and the respect of the kids, I too would have been splashed and dunked along with each of them. But, the calm water is also a time for relaxing. Soon, we are holding onto one another's inner tubes to form a loose circle. As we drift idly along, one of the kids tells a ghost story.

Well, it looks like the kids have helped me write this chapter. Thanks, guys.

▶ **Note:**
Always call on the day you plan to go tubing to get current hours of operation and river conditions.

The picnic grove is close to the parking lot, a welcome sight for ravenous "tubers." After changing into dry clothes (changing rooms are available), we grab the picnic basket from the car and head for a table.

There is an abundance of trees here which means the tables are sometimes dusted with debris and the ground littered with soggy leaves. But, once I cover both the table and my feet, I am comfortable. The kids don't notice anything except the food, and I realize the occasion does not demand a luxurious area—just a convenient one. After eating, we feel warm and content for the drive home.

In retrospect, I am suggesting something heartier than snack food for this picnic, no matter what time of day, especially if there are older kids and teenagers in the party. River tubing is exhilarating and we worked up an appetite.

▶ What's In Our Picnic Basket?

Grinders

Bags of chips

Soda

▶ **Brendan's Beef Jerky**

Brendan's Beef Jerky

(Courtesy of Brendan McCarthy)

This is my grandson's creation and he agreed to share the recipe with my readers.

1 three-pound London Broil steak
2/3 cup Al Steak Sauce
1/3 cup Worcestershire sauce
1 teaspoon black pepper

1 teaspoon onion powder
1 teaspoon garlic powder
1 zip lock bag, gallon size

▶ Remove all visible fat from steak. Slice lengthwise into 1/4-inch strips. Place strips into a gallon size baggie.

▶ Mix rest of ingredients: steak sauce, Worcestershire sauce, pepper, onion, and garlic powder and add to bag. Seal bag and rotate until all meat is coated with sauce.

▶ Marinate in refrigerator for 7-10 hours.

▶ Remove meat from bag and lay strips out on a layer of paper towels. Place another layer of paper towels on top and blot off remaining marinade.

▶ Line bottom of oven with aluminum foil.

▶ Drape beef strips over oven racks. Heat oven to 175 degrees F. Prop door open 1 or 2 inches with a metal rolling pin or meat mallet.

▶ Cook for 8-10 hours or until meat is dry and bendable but does not break.

▶ When cool, store in gallon size zip lock bag. Will keep up to 2 weeks.

▶ Yield: 16-20 pieces depending on length and thickness of beef.

Hammonasset Beach State Park
Madison

Years ago, it was enough to have two miles of sandy beach on which to stretch out on a blanket, rub on suntan lotion and soak up the sun. It was also enough to swim in the sound, read a good mystery, build a sand castle with the kids, or stroll along the beach looking for seashells and stones. And, always, at some point in the day, to picnic. Ah, the memories.

Today, it is about rediscovering an old state park with new ideas. It is about finding the same familiar beach scene we expect and love, while uncovering subtle improvements and fresh diversions. At West Beach, we can enjoy the coastline while walking the boardwalk (almost three lengths will net us a mile) or while biking a one and one-quarter mile trail. At East Beach, we can get back to nature on any one of three self-guided nature trails, and learn the fascinating history of this area at the nature center. While there, we might visit the small aquatic animals inside the building or stroll out to the back to sit next to the Friendship Pond.

Hammonasset Beach State Park was named "for the spirit and memory of the Hammonasset tribe who originally inhabited this land." The Park was purchased in 1919 to become Connecticut's third state park. Both the Meigs Point Nature Center and "The Friends" website provide an amazing history of Hammonasset, beginning with the Ice Age, about 10,500 B.C.

The three nature trails are diverse and scenic, and have much to teach us.

Hammonasset Beach State Park

Address: 1288 Boston Post Road, Madison, CT 06443.
Telephone: (203) 245-2785.
Website: www. ct.gov/dep/site. Click Outdoor Recreation; click State Parks & Forests; click Quick Links.
Open: Year-round 8am to sunset.
Parking fees in season: W/E & Holidays: CT residents $10; non-residents $15; after 4 pm $5. Weekdays: CT residents $7; non-residents $10; after 4 pm $5.
Meigs Point Nature Center: (203) 245-8743
Open: Open: Apr–June Tue–Fri 10–5; July–Aug Tue–Sun 10–5; Sept–Oct Tue–Sat 10–5; Nov–Mar Tue–Fri 10–4. Off-season hours may vary depending on school programs.
Friends of Hammonasset Website: www. hammonasset.org. Click on Nature Center.
Admission: Free
Directions: From Interstate 95, Exit 62 to Hammonasset connector. See signs for Park entrance.

Moraine Trail is perhaps the most popular of the three trails because of its location at the very easterly end of the beach, almost across from Meigs Point Nature Center and near the boat launch. An interpretive guide is available in the box at the trailhead. A moraine, an irregular mass of unstratified glacial drifts, is very much in evidence, especially boulders. According to the guide, the moraine here is rare because its internal composition can easily be seen. Other highlights of the trail are sand dunes, dune grass, beach rose, eastern red cedar, and—careful!—poison ivy. And this is just at Station 1! The observation platform at Station 5 provides much historical commentary about the area, and Station 8 ends at a salt marsh. Everything in between is equally as appealing, but more so because of the proximity to and view of Long Island Sound and the Hammonasset River.

Willard Island, which can be accessed behind Meigs Point Nature Center, has 13 stations of interest, including a salt marsh, fruit trees (the property was once used for agriculture), and an Observation Platform. The interpretive guide located at the beginning of the trail helps identify points of interest and lists some of the wildlife that can be found here.

Cedar Island is a third walking trail, but at the time of our visit the interpretive guide was in the process of being printed.

Meigs Point Nature Center is packed with the information and exhibits that one would expect in a beach nature center: preserved animals in a natural setting, aquariums labeled salt water – rocky shore; brackish water – marsh; fresh water – pond; and, salt water – sound. Reptiles and amphibians also live here. Downstairs is a Discovery Room and touch tank with turtles, fish, skates and sea stars.

The Center, established in 1972, continues to grow and thrive, thanks to "The Friends of Hammonasset" founded in 1999. This organization has been instrumental in the Center's recent renovations and refurbishing, thereby allowing it to lengthen its open season and offer new science and nature programs to the public as well as ongoing projects for school age children. Special events, such as the Native American Awareness weekend, Star Gazing, and Kite Festival, are scheduled at various times during the year.

On the day we visit we join an early morning nature walk. Among the sights along the trail are a tidal pond with a small blue heron, osprey, and lots of wildflowers, plants, and birds, all of which Russ Miller, the director of the Nature Center, identifies for us.

Later, we discover the Friendship Pond and Butterfly Garden in back of the building. Sitting on a bench next to the pond and watching the monarch butterflies feels almost surreal in the middle of a beach day. Many of the butterflies have been tagged and found to have migrated as far away as Mexico. If we are still, one might alight on our shoulder and enjoy the sunshine with us!

Hammonasset is Connecticut's largest and most frequently visited state park. This year, we will be counted as two of the 1.7 million people who visit annually.

▶ The Picnic

Where to picnic? Ah, that is the question. Not, is there a place to picnic, but which setting shall we choose?

We can choose a picnic table set in pine groves on either side of the entrance from the parking lot to West Beach, or a table that is spread out beyond the trees for sunshine.

The best-kept secret is the picnic area just across the street from East Beach, in back of the Nature Center, where several tables sit on a green lawn near the Friendship Pond and Butterfly Garden.

In season, there are picnic tables on the deck at the East Beach bathhouse where there is also food and drink. (Other concession stands are located just west of the entrance to West Beach, and further east, before the East Beach bathhouse).

Picnic shelters at various locations are suitable for groups and can be rented from Memorial Day through Columbus Day.

Finally, there are the two miles of sandy beach where we still like to spread a blanket, place our cooler and picnic basket on corners to keep it secure, and unpack our lunch. And, hope that no little kids run by kicking up sand while we are eating. But, if that does happen, there is something so magnetic about eating lunch in the beach air with a view of the unending sound, it's even worth a few grains of sand in the salad.

▶ What's In Our Picnic Basket?

Snacks

▶ **Spiedies**
Pickles and Olives
Cookies
Yogurt

Spiedies

(Courtesy of Karen Hoke)

Spiedies, a sandwich originating in the Binghamton, NY area in the 1920s, is made from pieces of marinated, grilled meat traditionally served in an Italian hard roll or folded slice of Italian bread. It is thought that lamb was the original meat used, with chopped mint added to the marinade.

Marinade:
2/3 cup olive oil
1/2 cup balsamic vinegar
(or 1/4 cup balsamic and 1/4 cup
red wine vinegar)
5 large cloves garlic, crushed
1 tablespoon lemon juice
2 teaspoons dried oregano

2 teaspoons salt
1 tablespoon dried crushed
basil leaves
1 tablespoon dried crushed parsley
1 teaspoon onion powder
1 teaspoon course ground
black pepper

- 2 pounds meat of your choice, cubed (lamb, pork, beef, chicken, etc.).

- Combine the marinade ingredients. Reserve 1/3 cup of the marinade and refrigerate.

- Place the balance of marinade and the cubed meat in a covered non-metal container or large zipped plastic bag. Refrigerate at least 12 but not more than 48 hours (less for chicken).

- Grill skewered cubes of meat until just done (do not overcook). Place meat in the roll or bread, which has been spread with butter or mayonnaise.

- Makes 6 sandwiches.

Option: Drizzle reserved, warmed marinade over the meat, or add grilled or sautéed peppers, onions, or mushrooms to the basic recipe. Pita pockets may be used in place of Italian bread.

Travel Tip

I found that when carrying Spiedies to a picnic site, buttered oblong rolls work best. Do not use the reserved marinade, but do try the sautéed peppers and onions (Yum!) Spiedies are equally good served warm or cold. Serve warm (or room temperature) by making sandwiches with the warm meat. Wrap in aluminum foil and pack in an insulated bag or container. Eat within two hours. Otherwise, store the cooked meat and sautéed vegetables in the refrigerator until leaving for picnic. Transfer to cooler and prepare at picnic site.

Thimble Islands Cruise
Branford

What do President Howard Taft, Captain Kidd, and Tom Thumb have in common? Ties to the Thimble Islands, of course. Two of these well-known men only came for a visit—one long enough to bury his treasure, and the other long enough to visit Little Miss Emily, a midget performer with the Barnum & Bailey Circus. The third man built a three-and-one half story twenty-seven room English Tudor home on one of the islands.

Can you match up the three men with the names of the islands they were associated with? Treasure Island is an easy guess, but how about Cut-in-Two Island and Davis Island?

Ever wonder what's in a name? Well, we read that the Thimble Islands were named for a wild thimbleberry that grew there. But the origin of the names of each island, such as Money Island, Horse Island, or Little Pumpkin Island, will have to be discovered on the forty-five minute narrative boat tour.

Mother-in-law Island provides one of the most entertaining stories of how an island was named. The legend goes that a young couple got married on one of the islands. They rowed away to a nearby deserted island for a camping honeymoon, only to be intruded upon by the groom's mother-in-law. The newlyweds, determined to find privacy, left in the middle of the night, taking both rowboats and leaving the bothersome meddler stranded on the rocky shore for three days!

Reality or myth? That is up to each person to decide. But one thing is certain—the Thimble Islands tour will amuse and delight both adults and children. The tours leave from Stony Creek, a coastal community in Branford, but unfortunately (or fortu-

Thimble Island Cruise, Stony Creek Town Dock

Directions: From Hartford take I-91 south to I-95 north, Exit 56. Go right, and proceed 2 miles to stop sign at intersection. Continue straight, pass under Train Bridge, and follow signs for Town Dock.
Parking: Park where permitted. Parking spaces are limited so allow for extra time.

Sea Mist:
Telephone (203) 488-8905.
Website: www.thimbleislandcruise.com.
Cost: Adults $9; Seniors $8; Children $5.

Volsunga IV:
Telephone (203) 481-3345.
Website: www.thimbleislands.com.
Cost: Adults $9; Seniors & Students $8; Children $5.

Schedule: Both boats have cruises scheduled from May through October; however, the times vary for both depending on the month and day of the week. Check websites for current information.

nately if you are a resident of one of the islands), visitors are not allowed to set foot on land. All the islands are owned by approximately 125 families who enjoy isolated summers on their own Shangri-la.

▶ The Picnic

After the boat tour, we are in no hurry to rush away from the charming village of Stony Creek. A small, oceanfront park adjacent to the dock is a serene setting for a picnic lunch.

Two people might choose, as we do, to sit on one of the wooden benches for a casual picnic. With children, you will be inclined to lay a blanket on the grass or the sandy beach.

Although there is a bustling of activity all around us, our view provides a soothing ambiance. Perhaps it is the colorful boats bobbing in front of us, or could it be that our thoughts are still on the Thimble Islands—perhaps with Captain Kidd or a mother-in-law?

▶ Skewered Shrimp and Vegetables

Bread or Rolls

Lemon Squares

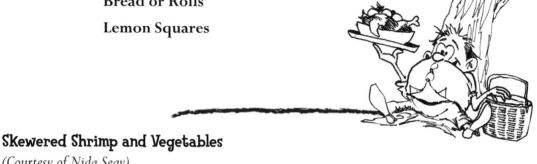

Skewered Shrimp and Vegetables

(Courtesy of Nida Seay)

During a Florida visit, a friend invited me to her stir-fry demonstration for the neighbors in her condominium complex. I enjoyed watching her ease in the kitchen and hearing her assurances, "It's really easy." The great taste was enough for me to try it myself when I returned home. Despite the several steps in the kitchen to prepare this recipe, it really is easy, and so worth the effort when you need a special dish.

SHRIMP:

1 pound (about 16) uncooked jumbo shrimp	2 tablespoons lite soy sauce
1/4 cup olive oil	2 tablespoons sugar
3 cloves garlic, finely chopped or minced	1/2 teaspoon salt
	1/2 teaspoon pepper

▶ Peel and devein shrimp. Paper towel dry. Combine rest of ingredients in a bowl. Add shrimp and toss to coat with sauce. Cover bowl and marinate in refrigerator for 30 minutes, turning to coat once.

▶ When ready, remove shrimp from marinade. Sauté in frying pan for 2-3 minutes or until pink, stirring constantly. There should be enough oil left on the shrimp, but if necessary add a small amount of additional oil while sautéing.

▶ Remove from pan, cool slightly, and refrigerate in covered bowl.

VEGETABLES:
carrots, peeled and sliced into 1/4-inch thick rounds (16 pieces)
16 broccoli florets
16 mushrooms caps
garlic and onion powder
ground ginger
salt and pepper
sugar (optional)

▸ In clean frying pan, heat 1/2 teaspoon olive oil over medium heat. Add carrots and a light shake of salt, pepper, garlic powder, onion powder, and ground ginger. Sprinkle with sugar. Cook until tender crisp (about 6-7 minutes) stirring frequently; lower heat to medium-low and add mushrooms. Continue cooking and stirring frequently for another 6-7 minutes until mushrooms are tender but still firm. If necessary, add a small amount of additional olive oil. When done, remove from pan, cool slightly and refrigerate in a covered bowl.

▸ In clean frying pan, heat 1/2 teaspoon olive oil over medium heat. Add broccoli, salt and pepper, and a little sugar, if desired. Cook several minutes. If pan gets too hot, turn heat to medium-low; add more oil if needed. Cook until fork tender. Remove from pan, cool slightly, and refrigerate in a covered bowl.

▸ Before leaving for your picnic, thread one each: shrimp, carrot, mushroom, and broccoli onto 6-inch skewers. Wrap, and carry to picnic site in a cooler. Serve cold as appetizer or main dish.

▸ Alternatively, carry three separate containers of shrimp, carrots and mushrooms, and broccoli to picnic site in cooler. When ready, thread the items onto skewers to serve, or if you prefer to serve warm, heat on charcoal grill. Soak wooden skewers in warm water for 20-30 minutes prior to threading. Make sure the grill is not too hot and there is plenty of space between the grill and the hot charcoal. You can also heat on aluminum foil.

▸ Yield: 16 skewers containing one each: shrimp, carrot slice, mushroom cap, and broccoli floret.

Gouveia Vineyard
Wallingford

"Come visit us for a spell" is one of the examples in Webster's Dictionary for the word "spell." I looked it up when I got home after visiting Gouveia Vineyards, for a spell. Oh, and if you are curious as to how long a "spell" is, Webster defines it as "an indefinite period."

That's just fine with Joe Gouveia. One of Joe's fondest memories of growing up in a small town in Portugal is when all the neighbors came to his grandfather's vineyard to harvest the grapes, toast the wine, and socialize. Adults and children alike blended into the happy community and everyone stayed for a spell. This is the feeling that Joe wanted to re-create at his own vineyard in Wallingford. So, during the October grape harvest, 100% of the grape pickers are volunteers. Add a huge dose of hospitality, some lively music, and ladies stomping the grapes — yeah, I can almost picture Joe's memory of long ago.

Joe and his wife Lucy found the idyllic acreage right in Wallingford where they were living. The year was 1999. First, the planting of the vineyards, next the building of the home, then the winery and, soon after, an addition to the winery, an expanded tasting room with plenty of comfortable space for families, including kids, grandparents, extended family, neighbors, and friends. In fact, for anyone who finds pleasure in the relaxing art of sipping a glass of fine wine, socializing, and enjoying the view through walls of windows. And, if it's a Saturday evening, listening to live music.

Gouveia Vineyard

Address: 1339 Whirlwind Hill Road, Wallingford, CT 06492
Telephone: (203) 265-5526
Website: www. gouveiavineyards.com.
Open: Year-round Fri–Sun. Closed major holidays.
Hours: Fri & Sat 11–8; Sun 11–6
Location: From Hartford, Route 91, Exit 14, turn left at end of ramp onto E. Center St. Turn right onto Whirlwind Hill Rd. Approximately one-half mile on right. From New Haven, Route 91, Exit 14, turn left at end of ramp onto Woodhouse. At second light, turn right onto E. Center St. Turn right onto Whirlwind Hill Rd.

Wallingford may not be Joe's childhood home in Portugal, but this hilltop location, overlooking a magnificent sweep of woodland interspersed with fields and farms, is more than fine. Besides, the most important memory, that of a happy community, has already been defined here at Gouveia Vineyards.

▶ The Picnic

Ahhh!! This is paradise for picnickers.

On one side of the winery picnic tables are attractively spaced so you can savor the view of the colorful countryside, although picnickers are not above finding an equally desirable spot of lawn. On the other side, a seasonal canopy provides cover for the cement patio furnished with tables and chairs. The small pond in front of the building has a deck which comfortably holds four folding lawn chairs, plus picnic basket, cooler, and assorted bottles of Gouveia wine and whatever foods you are feasting on. I know this because I enviously chatted with some folks who were enjoying a summer afternoon doing just that. Oh, did I mention that these are only the outdoor picnicking options?

Inside, there is not one but two tasting rooms, each providing a different mood. The first is smaller and more intimate with a stone fireplace and several round tables. An adjacent room, much larger, is filled with glass-covered tables and comfortable chairs for more serious dining. It is interesting to observe folks as they arrive. They all seem to know, either by experience or instinct, what to do. Find a table for the picnic basket and cooler, go to the bar for the wine tasting and purchase of a bottle (or two) of their favorite, then head back to the table to sit for a spell and picnic.

What — no picnic basket? To make sure that no one goes hungry while enjoying Gouveia wine, complimentary snacks, such as cheese, crackers, salsa and chips, are always on hand.

▶ # White Beans, Chorizo Sausage & Mint
▶ # Shrimp Catalan

Spanish Cheese (I like Manchego)

Olives

Almonds

Crusty Bread

A Spanish Tapas Picnic

(Courtesy of Prudence Sloane, Radio & TV Food Show Host)

Tapas surely must be one of the most sociable of cuisines and is perfect picnic fare. Tapas are small dishes of food - just a bite - similar to hors d'oeuvres. The word 'tapas' means "to cover" and it was originally just a piece of bread, perhaps with a slice of ham placed on it, resting on top of a glass of wine or sherry. It basically kept the flies out of your drink! That simple cocktail nibble has grown into a great tradition in Spain, where a popular bar might offer as many as twenty small tapas, such as marinated vegetables, small sandwiches, turnovers, stewed meats, sautéed seafood and cured meats, all designed to accompany either dry sherry or wine.

For a Spanish tapas picnic feast all that's needed is one or more tapas dishes, some simple accompaniments such as cheese, olives and almonds, and crusty bread, the local wine and you've got a great picnic!

White Beans, Chorizo Sausage & Mint

This dish gets better the next day as the various flavors merge together. It is best served at room temperature. (Serves 4)

3 oz chorizo sausage, diced (chorizo is a spicy smoked pork sausage favored with paprika, garlic and spices. There is a Portuguese chorizo called Gaspar's which is easily found in most supermarkets)

▶ In a medium sauté pan sauté the diced sausage with a small amount of water for 5 minutes, or until the fat is released and the sausage is lightly browned. Remove the sausage and wipe the pan.

2 cups cooked small white beans
  (if canned beans are used, rinse first)
2-3 tablespoons extra virgin olive oil
4 scallions, diced (or 1 small onion)
2 teaspoons minced garlic

1/4 cup white wine
1 teaspoon anisette liquor (optional)
2 tomatoes diced
2-3 tablespoons chopped fresh mint
Salt & freshly ground pepper to taste

▸ Heat 1 tablespoon of the olive oil and add the scallions and garlic. Sauté for one minute. Add the white wine, anisette, tomatoes and cooked sausage.

▸ Cover and simmer for 5 minutes. Do not allow it to dry out. Add water if necessary. Add the beans and simmer until the sauce coats the beans.

▸ Remove from the heat and let it come to room temperature. Add mint and seasoning to taste. Drizzle the remaining olive oil right before serving.

▸ This can be made two days ahead and kept refrigerated. Bring to room temperature before serving.

Shrimp Catalan (Serves 4)

1 lb large shrimp
  (about 30-40 shrimp)
1/3 cup olive oil, separated
2 tablespoons chopped toasted almonds
1 teaspoon minced garlic

1 teaspoon paprika
1 tablespoon chopped parsley
1/2 plum tomato, seeded and diced
1 teaspoon coarse salt, if needed
  (taste shrimp first)

▸ Add 2 tablespoons of the olive oil to the pan. When the oil is just beginning to smoke, add shrimp. Sauté on medium-high heat until done (1-2 minutes).

▸ Add remaining ingredients and toss.

▸ Serve at room temperature with crusty bread.

> ▸ **Note:**
> Only 2 tablespoons of olive oil are needed to cook the shrimp. The remainder is a sauce to be soaked up by bread, if desired.

Haight-Brown Vineyard
Litchfield

They said it couldn't be done. Agricultural Universities from here to California thought that Connecticut's cooler climate would prove unsuitable for wine-making. Thankfully, Mr. Haight didn't listen, and in 1978, Connecticut's first winery was established.

Mr. Haight retired recently, and as we park our car at the new Haight-Brown Vineyard, we are wondering if any changes have been made. Not surprisingly, visitors are still welcome to take the "Vineyard Walk." When we reach the second floor landing, the first thing we notice on this chilly December day is a fire crackling in the stone fireplace. It would be tempting to sit on the relaxing sofa nearby with a glass of wine, but first, we are drawn to the other end of the room to admire the many food and wine gift baskets and other gift items.

There are even gourmet cheeses and chocolates stored in a small refrigerator. We discover that these two delicacies are being featured today with a special wine tasting in the Vine Room. On other Saturdays, it may be an Artist Reception with jazz, food, local art, and of course, the wine tasting.

At the new custom-built wine bar, we thoroughly enjoy sampling 9-10 vintage wines, noting the new trend for Connecticut wineries in charging a nominal fee for wine tasting. We are okay with this, especially considering the wine glass is ours to keep.

During our tasting, we recall the interesting wine cellar tours from years past, and how they gave us a greater appreciation of the technique of winemaking, and the artistry of the winemaker. You can take advantage of Haight-Brown's complimentary tours on weekends from May through December. Just contact the winery beforehand to get hours and make reservations.

Haight-Brown Vineyard

Address: 29 Chestnut Hill Road, Litchfield, CT 06759.
Telephone: (860) 567-4045.
Website: www.haightvineyards.com.
Open: Jan–Feb Sat & Sun only; Apr–Dec everyday except Mon.
Hours: Tue–Fri 11–5; Sat 11–6; Sun 12–6. Note: check website or call to confirm schedule.
Location: Look for Wine Trail sign at Intersections of Routes 8 & 118 continue traveling on 118 for 2-3 miles. Chestnut Hill Rd. will be on your left. Wine Trail sign also at intersection of Route 8 & 118. Haight-Brown is located 1 mile east of Litchfield Center off Route 118.

C hoose one of the picnic tables near the beginning of the Vineyard Walk, or place a picnic cloth anywhere on the expansive green lawn. A nice alternative is the small veranda upstairs where you will find several café tables overlooking the scenic vineyard. Either way, the ambience is perfect for your picnic accompanied by a glass of your favorite wine.

If the weather does not cooperate for your outdoor picnic, the Vine Room may be an option. Just check first to make sure an event is not scheduled.

▶ What's In Our Picnic Basket?

Favorite cheese and gourmet crackers

Green and purple grape clusters

▶ White Bean Chicken Chili

Corn bread

White Bean Chicken Chili

One day, cream style corn, bought in error, went into the pot instead of my usual whole-kernel corn. The result was a rich, creamy base that everyone liked.

2 tablespoons olive oil (separated)

1 cup (or large) onion, chopped

2 garlic cloves, minced

1 to 1-1/2 pounds white chicken cut into small bite-size pieces

1 packet (1.5-ounces) taco seasoning mix

1 cup water

1 can (14-ounces) artichoke hearts, drained and cut into eighths

1 can (14.5-ounces) diced tomatoes

1 can (15.5-ounces) cannelloni (white kidney) beans

1 can (14.75-ounces) cream style corn

- In fry pan, heat 1 tablespoon olive oil over medium heat. Add onion and sauté until soft, 2-4 minutes. Add garlic and sauté for an additional minute stirring constantly. Remove from heat.

- In saucepan, heat 1 tablespoon olive oil over med-high heat. Add chicken pieces and 1/2 teaspoon taco seasoning mix. Sauté until the chicken is no longer pink, about 5 minutes.

- Stir remaining taco seasoning and water into chicken; then add cooked onion and garlic. Bring to boil. Add artichoke hearts, tomatoes and beans. Lower heat and simmer uncovered for 20 minutes. Add corn and heat through.

- Serve with a dollop of sour cream, if desired.

- Yield: 8 cups

> ▶ **Note:**
> Whenever I make a receipe using a lot of canned goods I try to find ingredients with less sodium. For this receipe, I was able to find a taco seasoning mix with 40% less sodium and diced tomatoes with no sodium. Also, the many brands of artichoke hearts on the grocery shelf contain varying amounts of sodium, so if this is a concern, check the labels.

Travel Tip Transport hot chili in a good quality wide-mouth thermos.

Hopkins Vineyard
New Preston

There is a cosmopolitan feeling at Hopkins Vineyard, possibly because of its proximity to New York City. October especially seems to be a hubbub of activity, with additional tourist attractions, such as Kent Falls State Park and Cornwall Covered Bridge beckoning leaf peepers from Connecticut as well as from neighboring states.

Both the vineyard and winemaking operations are open for self-guided tours on weekends, but they may play second fiddle to the other activities here. The first floor of the renovated nineteenth-century barn contains two large connecting rooms. One room focuses on wine tasting, the other is devoted to bottles of wine and gifts for purchase, although a few gifts spill over into the tasting room as well.

The wine tasting includes eight selections and the wine glass with a Hopkins Vineyard logo. Today, however, we only want a taste of each of two wines in order to make a decision of which one to buy for our picnic. Originally, we are told that visitors can taste one wine at no charge, but when we ask for the second taste, they do not refuse.

Gift items include an array of wine and related accessories, like wine stoppers, unusual corkscrews, glasses, and wine bottle holders. The gift department goes a step further, however, with sweatshirts, baskets, and shelves of gourmet food and condiments. They even offer their own label on glass-etched collector's bottles of olive oil and balsamic vinegar. The creative array of items is both attractive and fun, whether one is buying or browsing.

Hopkins Vineyard

Address: 25 Hopkins Road, New Preston, CT 06777.
Telephone: (860) 868-7954.
Website: www.hopkinsvineyard.com.
Open: Jan–Feb Fri–Sun; Mar–Apr Wed–Sun; May–Dec everyday.
Hours: Mon–Sat 10–5; Sun 11–5. Daylight savings time: Sat 10–7; Sun 11–6; Closed Thanksgiving, Christmas and New Years Day.
Location: Look for Wine Trail signs at Intersections of Routes 202 & 45, Routes 45 & 341, and Routes 45 & Flirtation Ave.

After examining a few more gifts that have filtered upstairs, we find the lively Hayloft Wine Bar, where visitors can order a glass of wine and a cheese and fruit platter while sitting at tables and savoring the view.

▶ The Picnic

"A Jug of Wine, A Loaf of bread—and Thou" (Edward Fitzgerald) Fitzgerald could have been describing this picnic! Hopkins Vineyard supplies the wine, and we supply the loaf of bread—well, the recipe anyway. You need only invite "Thou" to accompany you.

After your wine tasting and selection of a bottle of wine to complement your lunch, head outside for a picnic treat. The setting is straight out of a country journal, influenced no doubt by the Hopkins Farm, which began operations on this site back in 1787.

A picnic area adjacent to the barn contains several tables surrounding a small pond with wetland wildflowers, and sometimes grazing cows adding to the country atmosphere. Make a quarter turn to toast Lake Waramaugh and the surrounding fall foliage, considered by many to be the most spectacular in the state.

One of our favorite wines here just happens to be Sachem's Picnic, but we cannot say for certain that it isn't because of the intriguing name. A check into the origin tells us "the name of the wine recalls the early days of the family hotel named Sachem, and of summer guests enjoying picnics by the shores of Lake Waramaugh." We'll toast to that!

Cut-Up Veggies and Favorite Dip

▶ Sandwiched Meat Loaf

Cantaloupe Slices

Apple Pie

Sandwiched Meat Loaf

(Courtesy of Holly McCarthy)

This is a great meal for a winery picnic, because the two surprise ingredients, fruit and cheese, are in perfect harmony with a glass of wine. We think, however, that you will enjoy this sandwich so much you will be making it for many different occasions.

Loaf of Italian bread (12-ounce)

1 pound ground sirloin

1/2-1 cup well-packed breadcrumbs
  (from hollowed out Italian bread)

1 egg, slightly beaten

2 tablespoons finely chopped onion

1/2 cup applesauce

1/4 cup Parmesan cheese

1 teaspoon parsley

1/2 teaspoon marjoram

1/2 teaspoon salt

1/4 teaspoon pepper

4 ounces Cheddar cheese, sliced

2 tablespoons butter

2 tablespoons Dijon-style mustard

- Preheat oven to 350 degrees F.

- Cut loaf of Italian bread in half lengthwise. Hollow out each side leaving the walls about 1/2-inch thick. Spread the cut surfaces of the bread with butter and mustard. Cover to keep from drying out.

- Mix 1/2 cup of removed breadcrumbs with egg and add to ground sirloin in a large bowl. Add onion, applesauce, Parmesan cheese and spices, mixing well. If needed, mix in additional breadcrumbs (up to 1/2 cup) until mixture is firm enough to hold its shape.

- On a baking sheet, form the meat mixture into two ovals about the same size and shape as the loaf of bread. Place the cheese slices lengthwise on top of one oval, keeping in center of loaf. Press cheese slightly into meat. Cover with second oval pinching edges tightly together to keep the cheese from leaking out. Bake 50-60 minutes.

- After removing meat from the oven, immediately place inside the bottom loaf of bread and cover with the top. Double wrap with tinfoil and weight down for one-half hour to force the meat juices into bread. (2-3 cookbooks or a dictionary works well for weights.)

- Servings: 8–10

Travel Tip

Place the aluminum foil-wrapped bread in an insulated bag (or several layers of newspaper) to keep warm for up to two hours. If your schedule does not permit you to make this recipe just prior to leaving for your picnic, simply make it the night before. Refrigerate and serve cold.

Food Safety

This food safety guidance is provided by Diane Wright Hirsch, RD, MPH, a food safety educator with the University of Connecticut Cooperative Extension.

Picnics are a special treat on a nice day. The bacteria and other bugs that cause foodborne illness enjoy a good picnic too! So… give a little attention to some basic food safety rules and keep your picnic carefree.

Rule Number One: Wash your hands before preparing food and before eating. Hand sanitizing wipes or gels are useful.

Rule Number Two: Keep cold foods cold. Start with chilled ingredients when making salads or sandwiches. Refrigerate peeled fruits and vegetables and prepared foods for at least two hours before packing in a cooler to go. Use bags of ice or frozen ice packs to keep the temperature in your cooler at 41°F or below. Use several large ice packs and place them between layers and on top of food. Bacteria love to multiply when it is warm. The temperature in your trunk can reach over 150°F. Keep the cooler in the seating area of your car. When you get to your destination, place the cooler under a shade tree.

Rule Number Three: Keep hot foods hot. Be sure to eat them within one or two hours. You can store hot foods in their own cooler as well. Wrap hot foods well in foil and several layers of newspaper or towels and put them in a cooler designated for hot foods only. They will stay hot for a few hours this way.

Rule Number Four: Grill safely. When grilling meats, fish and poultry, there are two safety tips to keep in mind. First, do not cross-contaminate. Raw meat, fish and poultry can be the source of many foodborne bacteria. Keep raw foods away from ready-to-eat foods such as buns and salads that might be served with them. The plate, tongs and spatula you use to transport these raw foods to the grill can all be contaminated with bacteria. So, be sure to use clean utensils to remove the cooked food from the grill.

If you marinated raw foods before cooking, the marinade is now contaminated. Throw it out. To use the marinade as a sauce when serving, make a double recipe and set aside half for the sauce.

Cook meat, poultry and fish thoroughly to kill any of the foodborne bugs that can make you sick. Use a food thermometer to check the temperature before you remove food from the grill. You cannot tell if meat or poultry is done just by looking at it! The USDA recommends these safe end cooking temperatures:

Whole poultry - 180°F; breasts - 170°F
Hamburgers - 160°F; ground poultry - 165°F
Fish, beef, veal, and lamb steaks, roasts and chops - 145°F
All cuts of pork - 160°F; hot dogs - 165°F
(Also, you might be tempted to partially cook poultry or meat and finish it off on the grill later—this is not a safe practice!)

Rule Number Five: Throw it out. In most cases, it is the best way to handle leftover picnic food. Often it has been touched by many hands and exposed to warm temperatures for more than an hour or two. Some types of bacteria make toxins that cannot be cooked away. Reheating picnic foods that have been in the temperature danger zone (41°F to 140° F) for too long will not make it safer.

TRIP INDEX

RECIPE INDEX

About the Author

Writing has been a part of Jan's life since age nine, when she submitted a poem to the children's poetry section of the Hartford Times newspaper and promptly received her first rejection. But, what a rejection — a hand-written letter from the poetry editor encouraging her to continue writing! As an adult, Jan founded the Open Circle Writer's Group and is a member of Connecticut Authors and Publishers Association.

Along with writing, Jan has long had a passion for day tripping. "There is no greater enjoyment than going on an adventure. For me, that means scouring the state looking for exciting new places to be discovered." Jan enjoyed many years of designing special outings for friends and family before embarking on the biggest adventure of her life — writing and publishing a day tripping book.

The author would love to hear from readers with questions or comments. Write to her at: Hillside House Publishing, P. O. Box 1431, Glastonbury, CT 06033 or e-mail her at Jan@cruisingconnecticut.com.

Check out Jan's website at:
www.cruisingconnecticut.com